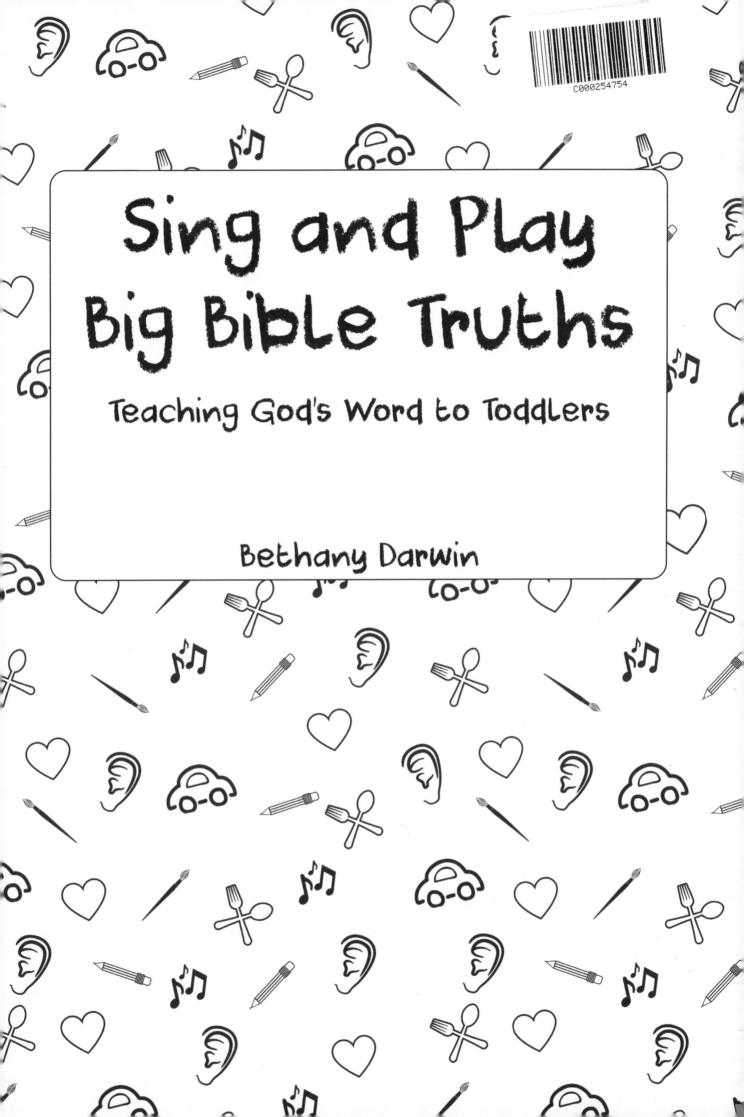

Sing and Play Big Bible Truths

Teaching God's Word to Toddlers

Bethany Darwin

C000254754

For Obadiah.
I pray you grow to
Love God and His Word
more and more
every day.

Contents

10 9 8 7 6 5 4 3 2 1
Copyright © Bethany Darwin 2020
ISBN: 978-1-5271-0560-7

Published by Christian Focus Publications,
Geanies House, Fearn, Tain, Ross-shire,
IV20 1TW, U.K.

All images are under license and edited from
Canva stock images

Cover design by Daniel van Straaten
Printed and bound by Bell and Bain, Glasgow

MIX
Paper from
responsible sources
FSC® C007785
FSC
www.fsc.org

Scripture quotations are taken from the HOLY BIBLE, NEW INTERNATIONAL VERSION®, NIV® Copyright © 1973, 1978, 1984, 2011 by Biblica, Inc.™ Used by permission. All rights reserved worldwide.

All rights reserved. No part of this publication may be reproduced, stored in a retrieval system, or transmitted, in any form, by any means, electronic, mechanical, photocopying, recording or otherwise without the prior permission of the publisher or a licence permitting restricted copying. In the U.K. such licences are issued by the Copyright Licensing Agency, 4 Battlebridge Lane, London, SE1 2HX. www.cla.co.uk

Free licence is given to copy activities pages for personal and class use only. Unauthorised copying and distribution is prohibited.

Safety Considerations

The activities in this book are designed with toddler hearts and hands in mind. Plus, every activity is designed to help you (parent or teacher) point these little hearts to Christ, which means they are meant to be done together. As you read on, you'll find activities that involve cooking and tasting various foods, creating crafts with glue and paint, splashing in water, exploring the neighborhood, singing and more.

Safety always needs to come first when doing activities with your toddler and you know your toddler's abilities and needs better than anyone else.

Here are some safety guidelines to consider:

1. All activities that involve the use of a knife or the stove should be done by adults with toddlers safely watching from a distance.

2. With the incidence of childhood allergies on the rise, it is possible that your toddler may be allergic to one of the foods listed in an activity. Please substitute for an ingredient that your child enjoys.

3. Please remember that all foods can potentially be choking hazards for young toddlers and all snacking activities need to be carefully supervised.

4. Some activities require the use of scissors. These activities often instruct the parent to do the cutting before the activity. If you are cutting with scissors around your toddler, please use care and keep scissors (and all sharp objects) out of the reach of your toddler's grasp.

5. For activities that use paint or glue, carefully supervise your toddler. If your toddler is still in the 'mouthing' phase, you may wish to substitute 'taste safe' alternatives. Recipes for 'taste safe' paint and glue can easily be found online and made with kitchen staples.

6. Water activities also require close supervision to ensure your toddler's safety. This close supervision provides more time for conversation.

Stay safe and have fun learning God's Word together!

Foreword

You only get to raise your children once. I tried to remind myself of this often when our two girls (now adult believers and adult friends to us) were little. Those days with them, as they grow and develop, are precious and irretrievable. Honestly, these are some of the best years of life and the joy and responsibility to make the most of their time with you matters much.

In our case, Jodi (my wife) began homeschooling our daughters when our older (Bethany) was in the 3rd grade. We had previously opposed homeschooling but seeing how much time Bethany was on the bus, and how little time was left in a day after school, gymnastics, music, and homework, I recall saying to Jodi, "Bethany's schedule is looking like mine!" (busy, that is). So, we pulled her out of school, and Jodi took upon herself the sober responsibility of teaching her at home. What a joy this was. She, and then Rachel who followed a few years later, learned and grew, and did so with relative ease and fun. Along with normal school subjects, Jodi led them in memorizing Scripture and learning a "hymn of the month," as well as Bible lessons and regular Bible reading.

Yet, as they grew, I wanted to develop a specific avenue into their spiritual lives that needed to be consistent and meaningful. I recall driving home from teaching seminary classes thinking what a joy it was to teach prospective pastors, and yet how could I be more involved in the spiritual development of my own daughters, as their dad? One night as we were putting them to bed, it occurred to me that neither one of them was eager to go to sleep, and so I thought, why not take some time with them at bed time to talk about "big truths" of God, Christ, sin, salvation, the gospel – truths that had the potential of shaping all of the rest of their lives, as the Holy Spirit worked in their hearts. Well, this led to many evenings, over several years, of spending 10 to 15 minutes with each of them at their bed time, thinking through glorious truths of the Christian faith. I always started with some verse from Scripture, so they could see that we form our conceptions of what is true and right from what the Bible teaches. What a joy, as their dad, to see them learn and grow, in mind and heart, as we traversed these many big truths together. Eventually, I wrote up these studies with my daughters in the book, *Big Truths for Young Hearts*.

Now parents of young children have at their disposal yet another tool, one that has great potential to grasp your children's minds and hearts, in such interesting and enjoyable ways. Bethany Darwin has an amazing gift for creatively placing big truths in settings that make it easy and very enjoyable for children to see and appreciate just what those truths are. The songs and activities she has devised will delight not only the children, but the parents who will be thrilled to be able to use such an attractive and reliable guide book. I am deeply grateful for the background of ministry Bethany brings to her labors of love, and I pray many will benefit much as these same glorious big truths impact yet another generation, for God's glory and the growth and joy of our children.

Bruce A. Ware
Professor of Christian Theology
The Southern Baptist Theological Seminary

Teaching Big Truths to Toddlers

I've always loved babies and young toddlers and started babysitting at a young age, but like many people, I saw them simply as cute and didn't think of using time with toddlers to impart knowledge, especially biblical truths. If anything, it would be the alphabet song or colors and shapes. And then, while in seminary, I did an internship at the on-campus preschool in their young toddler room. My philosophy of children's ministry was turned on its head in that toddler classroom. I suddenly realized that we needed to take every moment we had with every child entrusted to us (no matter how young) to proclaim the truth of the gospel and to teach the Bible.

This toddler class had seven children from 13 to 16 months and at first glance the room was what you would expect … cribs, high chairs, rocking chairs, toys, books, etc. But when you took a closer look, every detail in the room was designed to teach. I started my internship during a school-wide study on international missions and the room and all the materials were intentionally placed to teach the truth that we should go and tell all people about Jesus. That first week happened to be about missions in Africa. The books were all either Bible picture books, or African animals and scenery. The dolls had been wrapped in brightly colored fabric and placed alongside pictures of groups of Maasai women brightly arrayed in similar cloth. The toy kitchen area had pictures of African villages. There were large blocks that had been covered on all sides with Bible story pictures, Bible verses and pictures of African people. And everywhere in the room (all at toddler level) were Bible verses and reminders of the truths that the teachers were conveying to these young toddlers.

And, it wasn't just the environment that was teaching these toddlers, it was the teachers as well. As I observed the teachers, I noticed that every word they spoke was intentional. As a child would pick up a doll, they would speak of the people in Africa who have never heard of Jesus. As a child rolled the block to the side with the picture of Jesus on the cross, they would say, 'look it's Jesus on the cross. The Bible tells us that we need to tell everyone that Jesus died on the cross.' Yes, they also talked about the red dress that the Maasai woman was wearing or the round basket on the woman's head, but their speech was peppered with Scripture and these little ones were learning biblical truth all day long in this program. I was amazed and learned so much during the two months that I spent in that program.

For many people, the thought of teaching biblical truths to toddlers may seem like an impossible one. Aren't they too little to be learning about God? Surely they're too young to learn about sin and salvation? It may seem daunting to introduce such big truths at a young age, but what a better time to build a foundation of truth as your toddler is coming to understand the world around him. In every other area of your toddler's life he's coming to understand the basics – how to walk, how to talk, how to eat and how to be part of the world that he's come into. Think about it. Your child is a human sponge and he is absorbing everything around him. It's our job as parents and teachers to make sure that what he is absorbing is of the greatest spiritual benefit.

What could be more important during these times of foundational learning than introducing him to the truths of God and His Word? It's true that for the most part toddlers will not understand the words that we are using, but they also don't know what a circle is until we teach them. In the same way that we teach them circle and the color red, we can and should be teaching them about sin and the cross and sacrifice of Christ in our place.

Moses had it right in the book of Deuteronomy when he instructed parents to be teaching their children everywhere and at all times. Deuteronomy 6:7-9 says, "Impress them on your children. Talk about them when you sit at home and when you walk along the road, when you lie down and when you get up. Tie them as symbols on your hands and bind them on your foreheads. Write them on the doorframes of your houses and on your gates."

It's always been interesting to me to read Moses' instructions in these verses, because this is exactly how young children learn. Two thousand years have passed, but children still learn in the same ways. Children still learn best by repetition, familiarity and the modeling of the adults around them. Children will learn when they hear the same truth being repeated in the car, at the dinner table and in their bedtime prayer. And, they'll learn when they see reminders of these truths always before them.

This book is designed to help you introduce the BIG truths of the Bible to your babies and young toddlers in the way commanded in Deuteronomy 6; through repetition, familiarity and interactive activities. In no time at all, your toddler will be recounting the truth of the gospel to you in every day conversation as the gospel begins to take root in their young hearts. For each truth in this book, you'll find the following activities (shown by these icons):

 Big Truth Song – toddler-friendly big truth lyrics set to familiar nursery rhyme tunes with motions. Imagine instead of hearing about bus wheels over and over you could hear your toddler singing of Jesus coming to earth to die for our sin.

 Hear and Learn – a simple story with motions that can be repeated over and over. The stories are chosen as a representative text in the Bible where each particular big truth can be seen. For more stories to go along with each truth check out the appendix.

 Play and Learn – a quick game or activity that you can do with your toddler to reinforce biblical truth. The activities are just active play between you and your little one and occasionally make use of simple toys.

 Memorize and Learn – a short Bible verse with hand motions. Toddlers are at a phase of development where they are learning more and faster than at any other time in their life. Imagine the impact memorized Scriptures could have for the rest of their life.

 Eat and Learn – a themed snack along with ideas for reinforcing the biblical truth. What child doesn't enjoy a good snack? So, make the most of time when your child is sitting and focusing on food to review biblical truth. Plus, many of these snacks are simple enough for your toddler to help with the preparation, creating shared memories they and you will treasure for years.

 Create and Learn – a simple art or craft activity to help your toddler get hands-on with the big truth along with a coloring or activity page and a Bible verse coloring page. These activities span from simple coloring or pasting to more hands-on craft activities, but all are geared for little fingers. And, if a particularly messy activity is included, a less mess option is available for those days when you just don't want to give your toddler a third bath before lunchtime.

Ideas for how to use this book at home

1. Pull out or copy the song pages or Bible verse pages and place them around the house in places where you (and your toddler) will see them often. You may even want to print the story and activity page on the back and laminate them together to make them more durable and easier for you to use regularly. Or, take a picture with your phone and create an album you can refer back to often throughout the day.

2. Focus on a truth for a week at a time and then rotate back through them. The second or third time through the book, your kids will be excited to have the repetition and you'll be amazed at how much they remember.

3. Choose a time of day when your toddler is a captive audience. For many little ones this might be a meal or snack time. Try to avoid times that your toddler is especially tired.

4. Sing the song daily and repeat it throughout the day. For example, with the first week, "The Bible is God's Word," sing the song every time you see a Bible. The songs are catchy and simple and can be sung in the car, during a diaper change, at the dinner table or whenever you want to reinforce a biblical truth.

5. Choose a second activity to do each day. One day could be your snack day and the next your play day. You'll know best how your toddler will respond.

6. The stories are brief and can be told daily. After hearing the story a few times, you'll be amazed to see your toddler copying you as you do the motions and even starting to repeat the big truths back to you.

7. Remember that toddlers love repetition, so don't be afraid to do the same activity over and over again. This will help to cement the 'big truth' in their mind and give them confidence as they successfully complete each activity.

** For ideas on using these materials in a church or classroom setting, please see page 72.

The Bible is God's Word
(to the tune of "Farmer in the Dell")

The Bible is God's Word

The Bible is God's Word

It tells us all about God

The Bible is God's Word

additional verses ... swap out 3rd line

— It tells us that God made us ...

— It tells us that we all have sinned ...

— It tells us Jesus died for sin ...

Hand Motions:

- BIBLE – hands open in front like an open book
- GOD – point up
- WORD – cup hands around mouth like shouting
- US – point to self
- SIN – arms form X in front of face
- JESUS – arms out to side like cross

Hear and Learn: The Bible is God's Word

The **Bible** is **God's Word** (hold up a Bible).

The **Bible** is God talking to **us** (point to the kids).

The **Bible** is about **God** (point up).

The **Bible** is true (hold up a Bible).

The **Bible** is about what **God** has done (point up).

The **Bible** is about **God loving His people** (cross arms over chest).

The **Bible** is about **God saving His people** (arms out like a cross).

The **Bible** is **God's Word** (hold up a Bible).

The **Bible** teaches us about **God** (point up).

The **Bible** is **God's Word** (hold up a Bible).

The **Bible** teaches us that **we need Jesus** (arms out like a cross).

The **Bible** is **God's Word** (hold up a Bible).

The **Bible** teaches us that **Jesus died on the cross for our sin** (arms out like a cross).

The **Bible** is **God's Word** (hold up a Bible).

Play and Learn: Pass the Bible

Sit in a circle on the floor with your family. Play music and pass a Bible around the circle. When you stop the music, the person holding the Bible should stand up and you should say, "Thank you God for the Bible" or "The Bible is God's Word." Have your toddler repeat after you.

Memorize and Learn: Psalm 119:103

- **How sweet** – 2 thumbs up

- **are your** – point up

- **words** – hands open like holding an open Bible

- **to my taste,** – point to tongue

- **sweeter than honey** – 2 thumbs up

- **to my mouth.** – point to tongue

- **Psalm 119:103**

Eat and Learn: Sweeter than Honey

Make Honey Fried Bananas: Psalm 119:103 tells us that God's Word is sweeter than honey. To emphasize this point, make a special honey sweetened treat.

You will need: 2 bananas cut into ½ inch slices, 1 tablespoon butter or oil, 2 tablespoons honey, ¼ teaspoon cinnamon and ⅛ teaspoon salt.

Place butter (or oil), honey, cinnamon and salt in a non-stick pan over medium heat until butter melts. Swirl pan to evenly distribute the cinnamon and salt. Place banana slices in the pan. Cook for 3-4 minutes on each side. You want the bananas to brown but not burn, so watch them carefully. Allow to cool slightly before serving.

While kids eat their snack, read Psalm 119:103. Talk about how sweet their snack is and how the Bible says that God's Word is even sweeter. Talk about how when you eat something sweet you want to eat more sweet things because you enjoy them. Explain that the same thing is true with God's Word. The more we read the Bible and the more we learn about God, the more we want to read the Bible and learn about God.

Create and Learn: God's Word Megaphone

You will need: a paper cup, markers, scissors and stickers.

Remind your kids that the Bible is God's way of speaking to us and telling us about Himself. Have kids repeat truths about God in various voices: whisper, sing-song, shouting, like a lion, etc. Explain that you're going to make something that will remind them that God speaks to us through the Bible.

Before doing this activity, carefully cut the bottom out of a paper cup. Show your toddler how you can hold the bottom of the cup to your mouth and talk through it. Then, let them decorate their megaphone with markers and stickers.

After completing the megaphone, take turns using it to say things about God and His Word. Or, for really young toddlers, you can use the megaphone to tell them truths about God.

HONEY

How sweet are your words to my taste, sweeter than honey to my mouth. Psalm 119:103

How sweet
are your
words
to my taste,
sweeter
than honey
to my mouth.
psalms 119:103

God Made
Everything

God Made Everything
(to the tune of "London Bridge")

Go-d ma-de everything,

everything, everything.

Go-d ma-de everything.

God made all things good!

God made you and me ...
God made sun so hot ...
God made trees so tall ...
God made dogs that bark ...
God made fish that swim ...
God made elephants ...

Hand Motions:

- GOD – point up
- MADE – fists on top of each other, like building a tower
- EVERYTHING – point around
- GOOD – 2 thumbs up
- YOU & ME – point to someone & self
- SUN – look up with eyes shielded
- TREES – arms up like branches
- DOGS – bark like a dog
- FISH – hands together and wiggle like fish
- ELEPHANT – arm by face to make a trunk

Hear and Learn: God Made All Things Good

In the beginning only **God** (point up) was there. In the beginning there was nothing but **God** (point up).

God said, "Let there be **light!**" (shine flashlight) and there was **light**. **God** said it was **good** (2 thumbs up).

God said, "Let there be **sea** (make waves with arms) and sky!" **God** said they were **good** (2 thumbs up).

God said, "Let there be **land!**" (hands flat). **God** said it was **good** (2 thumbs up).

God said, "Let there be **trees** (arms up in the sky) and pretty flowers!" **God** said they were **good** (2 thumbs up).

God said, "Let there be a **sun** (big circle with arms) and a **moon** (head on your hands like sleeping) and **stars** (make twinkle stars with your fingers)!" **God** said they were **good** (2 thumbs up).

God said, "Let there be **birds** (flap your arms) and **fish** (put your hands together in front of you and wiggle like a swimming fish)!" **God** said they were **good** (2 thumbs up).

God said, "Let there be **animals!**" (bark, growl, etc.) **God** said they were **good** (2 thumbs up).

God looked at His **world** (big circle with arms) and said, "It is **good**" (2 thumbs up).

Then, **God** made **one** (hold up 1 finger) last thing. **God** made **people** (point at yourself). **God** made a **man** and a **woman** (point at yourself or to pictures of parents, man and woman). **God** (point up) **loved** (cross arms across chest) **them** (point to child). **God** looked at His **world** (big circle with arms) and said, "It is very **good**" (2 thumbs up).

Play and Learn: Creation Stop and Go

Play music and dance or move while the music plays. When the music stops, point to your toddler, something in the room or a picture and say, "God made the trees. God made everything" or "God made Hannah. God made everything."

Memorize and Learn: Psalm 19:1

- **The heavens** – big circles in air with hands
- **declare** – cup hands at mouth like shouting
- **the glory of God;** – point up
- **the skies** – big circles in air with hand
- **proclaim** – cup hands at mouth like shouting
- **the work of his hands.** – hands out in front
- **Psalm 19:1**

Eat and Learn: Star Sandwiches

You will need: a star cookie cutter and foods to be cut.

Psalm 19:1 tells us that the heavens declare the glory of God. Explain that this means that everything that God made tells us about God and points to God. Say the verse a couple of times with your kids and then ask what things they see in the heavens. Explain that the heavens are the sky. Talk about what we see in the sky in the daytime (sun, clouds) and what we see in the sky in the night-time (moon and stars).

Make your child's favorite sandwich and then use the star cutter to cut it into a star shape. If you have a smaller star cutter, you can also cut cheese or fruit (like apples) into stars for a whole starry lunch.

As you enjoy your star lunch, take time to thank God for the stars. Talk about what the stars teach us about God – God is the creator, God is big, God is powerful, etc.

Create and Learn: God Made Everything

You will need: blank paper, old magazines, scissors and glue sticks.

LESS MESS OPTION: Your smartphone or camera.

Remind your toddler that the Bible teaches us that God made everything. Go for a walk around your neighborhood and point out things that God made. Point to a flower and say, "God made the flowers." With older toddlers, ask questions like, "Did God make that tree?" and teach them to respond by saying, "Yes, God made everything."

Then, flip through some magazines and have kids help you find pictures of things that God made. As they find pictures, you can cut or tear them out and have the kids glue them onto a piece of paper.

LESS MESS OPTION: Take your phone or camera with you on your walk and take pictures of things that you find that God made.

Color everything that God made

The heavens declare the glory of God; the skies proclaim
the work of his hands (Psalm 19:1).

"the heavens declare
THE GLORY OF GOD
the skies proclaim
the work of his
hands." psalm 19:1

We Are ALL Sinners
(to the tune of "Mary had a Little Lamb")

We-e are all sinners,

all sinners, all sinners

We-e are all sinners

We don't ob-ey God.

Hand Motions:

• WE – point to someone & self

• ARE ALL – sweeping arms around to indicate all

• SINNERS – arms crossed in front of face

• DON'T – shake head NO

• OBEY – hug self

• GOD – point up

Hear and Learn: The First Sin

* **God** – point up

God made **everything** (big circle with your arms) in the world. **God** made **everything good** (2 thumbs up). The last thing **God** made was **people** (point to self and toddlers).

God put His **people** (point to child) in a beautiful **garden** (make tree branches with your arms). There was only **one** (1 finger up) rule in the **garden** (branches with arms). Don't **eat** (take a bite of a pretend apple) from the tree in the middle of the **garden** (branches with arms).

One day the **serpent** (wiggle hand like a snake) lied to the woman and said it was **good** (2 thumbs up) to **eat** from the tree. **God** said not to **eat** from it. The **serpent** said she should **eat** from it. The woman **listened** (cup hand by ear) to the **serpent** instead of **God**.

The fruit looked delicious. So, she **reached up** (reach up) and picked the fruit. She took a **bite** (pretend bite) and ate it. Then she gave some fruit to Adam, and he **ate** (pretend bite) it too. But as soon as they had eaten it, they knew something was **wrong** (sad face). They had disobeyed God. They had **sinned** (sad face). They **hid** (put arms in front of face) from **God**.

God asked them what they had done. Adam said that Eve made him do it (point to someone). Eve said the **serpent** made her do it. **God** said they had to be punished.

God made His **people** leave the **garden** and live far, **far away** (point far away) from Him. Before they left, **God** promised that one day He would come back and **rescue** them (hug toddler).

Play and Learn: Listen Follow

Remind your toddler that in today's story, people chose not to listen to God but listened to the serpent's lies instead. Play a simple game of giving instructions ... stop, go, walk, jump, close eyes, etc.

Memorize and Learn: Romans 3:23

- **For all** – make a sweeping motion to include everyone

- **have sinned** – make an X with your arms in front of your face

- **and fall short** – pat the ground with both hands

- **of the glory** – point to your big smile

- **of God.** – point up

- **Romans 3:23**

Eat and Learn: Forbidden Fruit Sauce

You will need: 2-3 apples, a knife, a cutting board, a pot, ⅛ teaspoon cinnamon, 1 tablespoon honey and a food processor/ blender.

Peel and roughly chop the apples. Place the apples and the cinnamon in a saucepan with enough water to cover the apples. Bring to a boil and let the apples simmer for 25-30 minutes until tender. Strain the water and transfer the apples to the food processor/ blender. Blend until smooth and stir in the honey. Stirring is a fun activity for toddlers. Let cool and serve.

While the apple sauce cooks, talk to your toddler about the story of Adam and Eve eating the fruit that God said not to. Explain that the Bible doesn't tell us what kind of fruit tree it was, but that we can use this apple sauce to remember that when Adam and Eve ate the fruit, sin came into the world.

Create and Learn: Apple Prints

You will need blank paper, an apple, a knife and some paint (preferably 2 colors).

LESS MESS OPTION: Nothing needed.

Remind your toddler of the story and how God told Adam and Eve they could eat from any tree except one. But Adam and Eve disobeyed God and ate from the tree.

Cut the apple in half and have your toddler either dip it into paint or use a paint brush to paint the apple. Then press the apple onto the paper. Allow your toddler to make several prints with the first color of paint. Then, remind them that there was one tree God said they couldn't eat from. Have them choose a second paint color and dip the other half of the apple into that color and make one print of that color apple. Display the picture somewhere your toddler will see it often, so you can remind them of the story and that we are all sinners.

LESS MESS OPTION: Go for a walk and collect leaves from various trees. Bring the leaves home and talk about all the different trees in your neighborhood. Have your toddler count the leaves and tell you their favorite. Remind them of the story and all of the trees in the garden and how God told Adam and Eve not to eat the fruit from one of the trees.

Color the tree. Then stick small circle stickers on the tree to represent fruit, while listening to the story.

For all have sinned & fall short of the glory of God.

romans 3:23

Only One
God

Only One God
(to the tune of "Row, Row, Row Your Boat")

One, One, One God,

There is only One!

There is no one that's like God.

God's the only God!

Hand Motions:

- ONE – hold up 1 finger
- GOD – point up
- THERE IS – hold left hand out flat
- ONLY ONE – hold up 1 finger
- THERE IS – hold left hand out flat
- NO ONE – shake finger on right hand like NO
- THAT'S LIKE GOD – point up with both hands
- GOD'S – point up with 1 hand
- THE ONLY GOD – point up with both hands

Hear and Learn: Elijah and the Prophets of Baal

* (God – point up) * (People – hug self)

God told His **people** that He would be their **God** and they would be His **people**. But the **people worshiped** (hands together praying) pretend gods instead of the **One** (hold up one finger) true **God**. **God** sent Elijah to tell the **people** to only **worship** (hands folded like praying) the true **God**. Elijah wanted the **people** to know that there is only **One** (hold up one finger) **God**.

Elijah told **people** who **worshiped** (hands together praying) fake gods to build an altar by piling up **stones** (pretend to pile stones). Elijah told them to ask their gods to light it on fire. All day long these **people** danced around the altar and called out to Baal, but Baal didn't answer, because Baal is a pretend god. Baal is not **God**. There is only **One** (hold up 1 finger) **God**.

Then, Elijah built an altar to **God**. He took 12 **stones** (take 12 blocks and build them on top of each other – counting as you go) and he built an altar. Elijah put wood on the altar. Elijah **poured 12 big jars of water** on the altar (pretend to pour and count to 12).

Elijah **prayed** (fold hands and bow head) to the **One** (hold up 1 finger) True **God**. Elijah asked **God** to remind the **people** that He is the **One** (hold up 1 finger) True **God**. Elijah wanted the **people** to see that there is only **One** (hold up 1 finger) **God**.

God sent fire down from heaven that burned up everything. **God** proved that He is the **one** (hold up 1 finger) true **God**! The people **worshiped** (hands together praying) **God**.

Play and Learn: Collect 12

Choose 12 each of several types of toys – blocks, cars, dolls, etc. Play with the toys with your toddler for a few minutes. Ask, "how many dolls do we have?" Count the dolls and say, "We have 12 dolls." Do the same thing with the cars or blocks. Remind them of the story and how Elijah used 12 stones to build the altar and poured 12 jugs of water over the altar. Have your toddler count with you. As you count, say "There are 12 dolls, but there is only 1 God!"

Memorize and Learn: Deuteronomy 6:4

- **Hear, O Israel:** – hand cupping your ear
- **The LORD** – point up with 1 finger
- **our God,** – wrap arms around self
- **the LORD** – point up with 1 finger
- **is one.** – hold 1 finger out in front of self
- **Deuteronomy 6:4**

Eat and Learn: Fruit Fire

You will need: 1 banana, a few sliced strawberries, ½ lime and a table knife.

Remind your toddlers how God showed His power through the fire in the story. Explain that you are going to retell the story using fruit and make a yummy snack to have together.

Start by cutting the banana into 12 pieces and stacking them up like the stones of the altar. Remind your toddler how Elijah built an altar to God. Then, squeeze the lime juice over the banana and remind them how Elijah had the people pour 12 big jugs of water on the altar. Then, place the sliced strawberries on top of the bananas (pointed ends up) and remind them how God sent fire from heaven to show that He is the only God.

As you enjoy your snack, talk about other stories in the Bible that show God's power: Moses and the burning bush, parting the Red Sea, Jesus walking on water, Jesus healing people, Jesus coming back to life, etc.

Create and Learn: Fire Paint

You will need: thick white paper, white crayons and watercolor paints with paint brush.

LESS MESS OPTION: A zip top bag, poster paint, tape

Remind your toddler of the story of Elijah and how God used him to show the people that He is the Only God. Use a white crayon to draw and color in (with a heavy hand) either the number 1 or the word God on a piece of thick white paper. Then, give your toddler watercolor paints and a paint brush and have them paint all over the paper. Hang them to dry and then show them how what you had written before can be seen even after they painted over it. With older toddlers, remind them of the story and how they poured water all over the altar, but God sent down fire and burned up everything on the altar (even all the water) and showed that He is the only God.

LESS MESS OPTION: Put several blobs of poster paint (red, orange, yellow) inside a gallon size zip top bag at different spots in the bag. Seal the bag and tape it to a surface. Let your toddler squish the paint around with his or her fingers to form the fire from the story. (This is a fun way to finger paint without the mess).

Elijah prayed to God and God answered by sending fire from heaven. Use red crayons or red paint to add fire to this altar.

Hear O ISRAEL: the LORD our God, the LORD is one.

deuteronomy 6:4

GOD

is good

God is Good
(to the tune of "Jingle Bells")

God is good,

God is good,

God is very good!

Everything that

God does

Shows that

He is good!

Hand Motions:

- GOD – point up
- IS GOOD – 1 thumb up
- VERY GOOD – 2 thumbs up
- EVERYTHING – sweep arms to indicate all
- THAT GOD DOES – point up
- SHOWS THAT – hand over eyes to help see
- HE – point up
- IS GOOD – 2 thumbs up

Hear and Learn: Water from a Rock

God (point up) led His people out of Egypt and **into the desert** (walk and wipe forehead).

God led the people through the **hot**, sandy **desert** (fan self).

The people got very **thirsty** (tongue out panting) as they walked. They said, **"I'm so thirsty"** (say in a whine).

Moses told the people that **God** (point up) is **good** (2 thumbs up) and that **He** (point up) was **taking care** (hug self) of them.

Moses **asked** (bow head to pray) **God** (point up) what he should do. God told Moses to take some of the leaders and **walk** (pretend to walk) ahead of the people. God told Moses that Moses should **hit the rock with his staff** (pretend to hit something) and water would come out of the rock.

God (point up) is **good** (2 thumbs up). **He** (point up) did just what **He** said **He** would do. Moses obeyed **God** and **hit the rock** (pretend to hit something) and water came flowing out of the rock. The people **drank water** (pretend to drink) and **thanked** (bow head to pray) **God** (point up) for giving them water.

Play and Learn: Water Play

Set up a towel on the floor with a deep tub with a small amount of water in the bottom of it. Provide a few things to play with in the water. Invite your toddler to come and play in the water. As they play, tell them that today's story is about God providing water for His people and that this story reminds us that God always takes care of His people.

Memorize and Learn: Psalm 107:1

• **Give thanks** – fold hands like praying

• **to the LORD,** – point up with 1 hand

• **for he is** – point up with your 2nd hand

• **good;** – 2 thumbs up

• **his love** – cross arms across chest like hugging self

• **endures forever.** – roll arms in front of body

• **Psalm 107:1**

Eat and Learn: Hidden Treat Rocks

You will need: 3 tablespoons butter, 3 cups mini marshmallows, 3 cups of puffed rice cereal, ½ cup dried blueberries, a pot and stove.

Melt butter in a saucepan over medium heat. Add the marshmallows and stir until melted. Take the pan off the heat and stir in the rice cereal. Allow the mixture to cool slightly until you can touch it. Take a small handful of mixture and form a cup shape in your hand. Add a few dried blueberries and then close it up to form a rock/ ball. Form all the rocks and allow them to cool. Once ready to eat, review the story and have your toddler pretend to be Moses hitting the rock with his staff ... open the 'rock' she hit to reveal the 'water' (blueberries) hidden inside. Enjoy the treat and thank God for providing for His people!

* Toddlers can help pour in the ingredients, but otherwise the mixture is very hot so they should only watch ... This may be a good time for them to color the picture.

Create and Learn: Glitter Water Bottle

You wIll need: a full water bottle (thick plastic or glass), glitter glue, glitter, small pebbles or plastic beads and a hot glue gun.

LESS MESS OPTION: A small empty water bottle.

Pour a small amount of water (one sip) out of the bottle. Squeeze (or let your toddler help squeeze) ½-¾ of a bottle of glitter glue into the water. Sprinkle in some glitter. Screw the lid on and shake vigorously for the glitter glue to combine well. Open the bottle and add the beads or pebbles. Hot glue the lid back onto the bottle. Toddlers can shake the bottle (under supervision in case the bottle comes open) and watch the glitter slowly sink to the bottom of the bottle. While making and playing with the bottle, remind children of the story of God giving His people water from a rock. Ask your toddler if they think they could get water out of the rocks inside the bottle.

LESS MESS OPTION: Take a small water bottle and go for a walk around the neighborhood. Allow your toddler to collect small rocks and put them in the water bottle. Once back home, put the lid back on the water bottle and repeat the story asking your toddler if they think they could get water out of the rocks in the water bottle.

God gave His people water from a rock. Complete the dotted line to draw a river coming out of this rock.

Give thanks to the LORD, for he is good; his love endures forever.

psalm 107:1

JESUS

Came to Earth

Jesus Came to Earth
(to the tune of "The Farmer in the Dell/Den")

Jesus came to earth,

Jesus came to earth,

He came to rescue

all God's people.

Jesus came to earth!

Hand Motions:

- JESUS – rock baby in arms
- CAME TO EARTH – make a big circle with arms
- HE CAME – rock baby in arms
- TO RESCUE – arms out like a cross
- ALL GOD'S PEOPLE – sweep arms to indicate all

Hear and Learn: Jesus is Born

* Jesus or Baby – rock a pretend baby

* God – point up

* People – point to kids

God promised to send someone to **rescue** (hug toddler) His **people**.

God's people were waiting and waiting and **waiting** (look at a clock or watch and wait for a few seconds). When would He come?

One day, the **time** (look at the clock) was right for Him to come. **God** sent an angel to tell a girl named Mary that she would have a **baby**. Her **baby** would be **Jesus**. **Jesus** was **God's** Son. **Jesus** was coming to **earth** (make a big circle with your arms).

When **Jesus** was born, Mary wrapped **Jesus** tightly in cloth and put him in a manger. This is where **animals like cows** (moo like a cow) usually ate.

God had sent His **rescuer** (hug toddler). Jesus had come to **earth** (make a big circle with your arms). **Jesus** was here to **rescue** (hug toddler) His people.

Play and Learn: Pass the Baby

Sit in a circle on the floor with your family and pass a baby doll around the circle while music is playing. When the music stops, the person holding the doll hugs it, then starts passing it again when the music starts again. While you play, remind toddlers that Jesus Came to Earth.

Memorize and Learn: John 1:14

- **The Word** – point up with one hand
- **became flesh** – pretend to rock a baby
- **and made** – pound fists on top of each other like building something
- **his dwelling** – use your arms to make a triangle above your head
  (like a house)
- **among us.** – point to each other
- **John 1:14**

Eat and Learn: Decorate Cupcakes

You will need: plain cupcakes, some frosting and fruit slices or candy that your child enjoys and a candle.

Allow your toddler to spread frosting on a cupcake using a plastic knife (or their fingers). Then let them choose some cut fruit (like strawberries) or candy to decorate the top of the cupcake. Finish by placing a candle in the cupcake. While working on the cupcakes, remind your toddler of the story and how Jesus came to earth as a baby to die on the cross in our place. Light the candle and sing "Happy Birthday" to Jesus before enjoying the cupcakes together.

Create and Learn: Footprint Manger

You will need: blank paper, washable brown paint, a paint brush, washable ink pad, a thin marker.

LESS MESS OPTION: Blank birthday card and crayons.

Paint one of your toddlers' feet with brown paint and press it onto the middle of the paper. The foot (sideways) becomes the manger with the big toe toward the top of the page and the little toe toward the bottom of the page. Use brown paint to paint legs on the manger in the shape of an X. Then, allow your toddler to place their finger on the ink pad and make two finger prints on top of the "manger". These prints are the faces of Mary and Joseph. You can then draw eyes and smiles on their faces and then their bodies. While you work with your toddler, remind them of the story.

LESS MESS OPTION: Give your toddler a blank birthday card and have them draw a birthday message for Jesus. After you and your toddler have made your cards, sing "Happy Birthday Jesus." Talk about how on Jesus' birthday we celebrate the best gift ever – that Jesus came to earth to die on the cross in our place.

happy birthday JESUS!

The WORD became flesh & made his dwelling among US.

john 1:14

JESUS
is the
SON OF GOD

Jesus is the Son of God
(to the tune of "Mary had a Little Lamb")

Jesus is the Son of God,

Son of God, Son of God.

Jesus is the Son of God.

He came down from heaven.

Hand Motions:

- JESUS IS THE SON – rock baby in arms
- OF GOD – point up
- HE – rock baby in arms
- CAME DOWN – squat down low
- FROM HEAVEN – point up

Hear and Learn: Jesus is Baptized

There was a man named John. **God** (point up) gave John a special job. John's job was to tell people that **Jesus** (arms out like a cross) was coming to **save** (hug self) God's people.

John told lots of people that **Jesus** (arms out like a cross) was coming. John told people to stop **sinning** (arms in X in front of face) and wait for Jesus. When people said they were sorry for **sinning**, John baptized them in the river.

One day, **Jesus** walked toward John. When John saw **Jesus**, he knew that this was the **Rescuer** (hug self). He knew that **Jesus** was the Son of **God**.

Jesus walked down into the river where John was and asked John to baptize him. When **Jesus** came up out of the water, something amazing happened. **God** spoke from heaven and said, "This is my **Son** (rock a pretend baby in your arms), follow Him."

Jesus is the **Son** of **God**.

Jesus is the **Rescuer**.

Jesus came to **earth** (make a big circle with arms) to **rescue God's** people.

Play and Learn: Does it Float?

Place a shallow basin of water on a towel and collect several small toys and place them around the basin. Sit on the floor with your toddler and hold up one toy at a time. Ask them if they think it will float (stay on top of the water) or sink (go under the water). Then, one at a time place the items in the water. After testing all of the items, allow your toddler to splash around in the water for a few minutes, while you remind them of the story of how Jesus came down to the river to be baptized by John the Baptist. Talk about how baptizing means dipping into water and pulling up out of the water. Remind them how John dipped Jesus under the water and when Jesus came out of the water God spoke and said, "This is my Son."

Memorize and Learn: Matthew 3:17

- **And a voice** – cup hands around mouth
- **from heaven said,** – point up
- **"This is my Son,** – rock a pretend baby in your arms
- **whom I love;** – hug yourself
- **with him** – rock a pretend baby in your arms
- **I am well pleased."** – smile big and point to your smile
- **Matthew 3:17**

Eat and Learn: Carrot and Dip

You will need: 1 avocado, 1 lime, a pinch of salt, a bowl, a fork, a spoon and carrots for dipping.

Remind your toddler that John was baptizing people in the river. John was dipping them into the water and pulling them up out of the water. Talk about how Jesus came to John to be baptized.

Explain that you're going to make a snack they can dip, to remember that Jesus was baptized. Scoop the avocado out into a bowl, squeeze the lime over it and sprinkle it with salt. Start mashing it with the fork and then allow your toddler to try. Or, once mashed, let him stir with the spoon. Sit together and dip carrot sticks into the avocado and enjoy them while reviewing the story again.

Option: if you don't think your toddler will eat carrots and avocado, offer anything they like to dip (fruit into yogurt, fries into ketchup, etc.).

Create and Learn: Water Painting

You will need: a paint brush and a cup of water.

Remind your toddler about how Jesus went down to the river to be baptized by John the Baptist. Talk about how John was telling people to be baptized and to stop sinning or disobeying God. Talk about how when Jesus went into the river, He would have gotten wet. Then, take your toddler and go outside with the paint brush and water. Allow your toddler to paint whatever they want with the water – the side of the house, the sidewalk, trees, etc. Notice how things get wet and then the sun dries them quickly.

JESUS IS THE SON OF GOD

Connect the lines to finish the river. Then count the footsteps as Jesus walked to the river to be baptized by John the Baptist.

And a voice from heaven said, "THIS IS my son whom I love; with him i am WELL PLEASED."

matthew 3:17

JESUS DIED on a Cross

Jesus Died on a Cross
(to the tune of "Mary had a Little Lamb")

Jesus died on a cross,

on a cross, on a cross.

Jesus died on a cross

to take away our sin!

Jesus died and rose again,

rose again, rose again.

Jesus died and rose again,

now we can live with Him!

Hand Motions:

- JESUS – rock baby in arms
- DIED ON A CROSS – arms out to sides
- TAKE AWAY – push away
- OUR SIN – big X with arms
- DIED – arms out like cross
- ROSE AGAIN – squat & jump up

Hear and Learn: Jesus Died on a Cross

* Jesus – arms out to the side like Jesus on the cross

* God – point up

Jesus came to **earth** (big circle with arms) for **one** (hold up one finger) reason.

Jesus came to **earth** to die on the **cross** (arms out to side).

God's people had **sinned** (use arms to form an X in front of your face). They had broken **God's** law.

The payment for sin was **death** (arms out to the side).

Jesus came to **earth** to die on the **cross** for **God's** people.

The soldiers put **Jesus** on a **cross**.

Jesus was in a lot of **pain** (make a pained face). Then, **Jesus** said "It is finished!" **Jesus** took one last **breath** (take a deep breath) and died. **Jesus** had died for **God's** people. Jesus had paid the price for **sin**.

Jesus' friends took Him off the **cross** and put Him in a tomb. **Jesus** was dead. **Jesus** had died to pay for **sin**.

Play and Learn: Build a Cross

Show your toddler pictures of a cross or draw a simple cross on a piece of paper. Then, work together with your toddler to build a cross out of blocks. As you build, retell the story and remind your toddler about Jesus dying on the cross. Building with blocks is also a good time to practice counting as you stack blocks together.

Memorize and Learn: 2 Corinthians 5:21

• **God made** – point up with both hands

• **him** – arms out to the side like Jesus on the cross

• **who had no sin** – arms crossed in an X in front of your face

• **to be sin for us.** – point to each other

• **2 Corinthians 5:21**

Eat and Learn: Cross Snacks

You will need: pretzel sticks or carrot sticks (whichever your child will eat).

Before snack time, use 2 pretzel or carrot sticks to form a cross on a plate. Ask your toddler what it is. Explain that it is a cross. Hold it up so it's standing and tell them that Jesus was put on a big wooden cross and that He died on the cross. Enjoy having a snack with your toddler while you review the story and the song.

Create and Learn: Finger Paint Cross

You will need: a piece of white art paper, some masking tape, scrap paper, finger paints.

LESS MESS OPTION: White paper, masking tape and crayons.

Cover your work area (table or floor) with scrap paper/ newspaper. Use masking tape to make the shape of a cross on a piece of white art paper. Place the art paper on the covered work area. Squeeze drops of finger paint randomly on the art paper and let your toddler have fun smearing it all over the page. Once finished, allow the paint to dry. Then, while reviewing the story with your toddler, carefully peel the tape off the page to reveal the shape of the cross.

LESS MESS OPTION: Do the same thing as above, except instead of painting, have your toddler scribble all over the page with different colors of crayons. You'll get the same effect when you remove the tape.

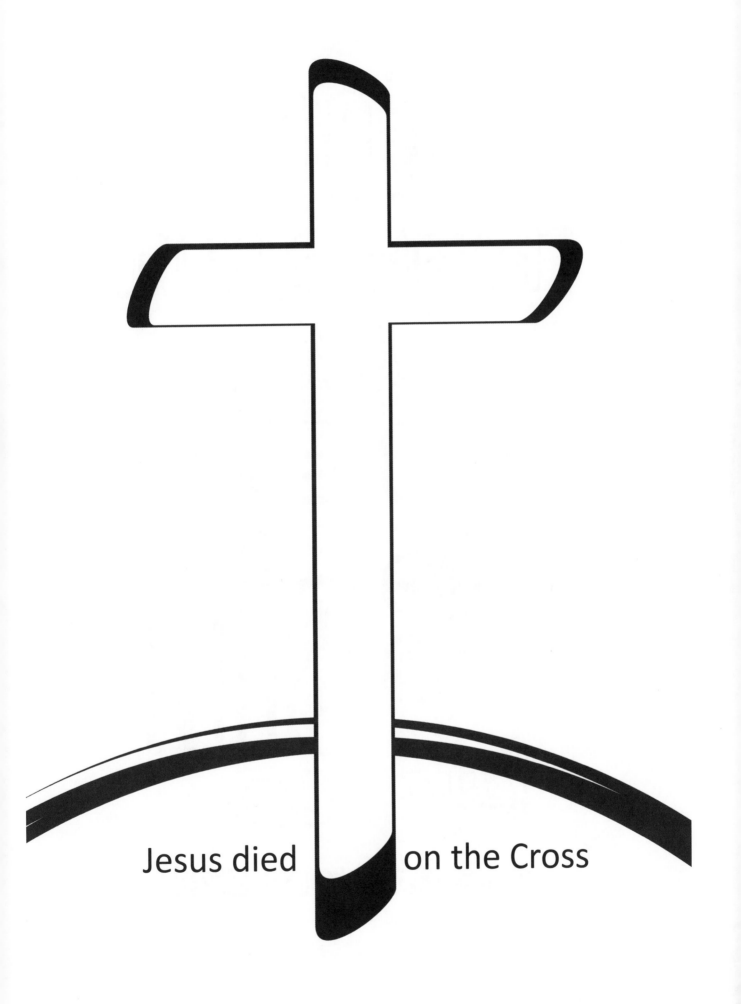

Jesus died on the Cross

God
MADE HIM
who had
no sin
to be Sin
for us.

2 corinthians 5:21

JESUS CAME back to Life

Jesus Came Back to Life
(to the tune of "The Wheels on the Bus")

Jesus came back to life,

back to life, back to life.

Jesus came back to life.

He came to life again!

Hand Motions:

- JESUS – rock baby in arms
- CAME BACK TO LIFE – both arms up in the air
- BACK TO LIFE – jump for joy
- HE – rock baby in arms
- CAME TO LIFE AGAIN – both arms up in the air

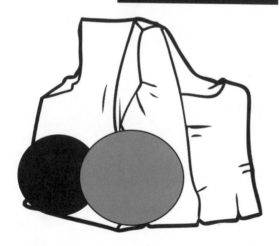

Hear and Learn: Jesus Came Back to Life

Jesus – arms out to the side like Jesus on the cross

Jesus came to **earth** (big circle with arms) for **one** (hold up one finger) reason.

Jesus came to **earth** to die on the **cross** (arms out to side).

God's (point up) people had **sinned** (cross arms in front of face) and the **sin** had to be paid for. The payment for **sin** was **death** (arms out to the side). **Jesus** came to **earth** to **die** on the **cross** for **God's** people.

When **Jesus** died on the **cross**, His friends put Him in a tomb. **Jesus** was dead. His friends were **sad** (make a sad face).

Three (hold up 3 fingers) days later, early in the morning, **Jesus'** friends **walked** (pretend to walk) to the tomb. The tomb was open. The tomb was **empty** (look inside something). **Jesus** wasn't there.

An angel told them that **Jesus** wasn't dead. Jesus was **alive** (jump up for joy).

Jesus died on the **cross**.

Jesus came back to **life** (jump up for joy).

Jesus is **alive!** (jump up for joy).

Play and Learn: Build a House

Build a small house with blocks. Place a small person or animal in the house and ask if the house is empty. Take it out and ask if the house is empty. Tell the kids that today's story is about a tomb that first had someone inside it and then was empty when Jesus came back to life.

Memorize and Learn: Matthew 28:6

- **He** – arms out to the side (cross)

- **is not here;** – shake head NO

- **he has risen,** – jump up

- **just as he said.** – hands by mouth like shouting

- **Come** – motion to come with both hands

- **and see** – hands over eyes like seeing far away

- **the place where he lay.** – lay head on hands and 'sleep'

- **Matthew 28:6**

Eat and Learn: Fruit Tombs

You will need: slices of pineapple without the core (fresh if possible) – about 1 inch (2.54 centimeters) thick, and grapes. Note: if you can't get pineapple, you could carve an apple slice.

Stand the pineapple slice up on the plate so you have an upside-down U shape. Show your toddler the opening in the pineapple. Tell them that after Jesus died on the cross, His disciples (His friends who followed Him) put Him in a tomb or a cave. The tomb had an opening like this. Encourage your toddler to put his finger in the opening. Explain that they closed the opening with a big rock while you roll the grape in front of the opening. Remind them of the story and how 3 days later when Jesus' friends came to the tomb, the big rock had been moved (move the grape) and the tomb was empty (look inside). Review the song while you have a snack of pineapple and grapes.

Create and Learn: Sad and Happy Faces

You will need: 2 paper plates, a wooden ruler, a pencil, washable ink pads, tape and a stapler.

LESS MESS OPTION: Smartphone or camera.

Remind your toddler how the people were sad when Jesus died on the cross and happy when He came back to life. Working on 1 plate at a time, sketch a simple happy face on the bottom of 1 plate and a simple sad face on the bottom of the other. Then, help your toddler place their finger on the ink pad and then make fingerprints along your sketch – eyes, nose and mouth. As they work on the sad face, have them make a sad face and talk about how sad Jesus' friends were when He died on the cross. As you work on the happy face have your toddler make a happy face and talk about how happy the disciples were to see Jesus alive again. Tape the ruler onto one of the plates, then staple the 2 plates together so your toddler can easily hold it and flip it around. Retell the story and have your toddler show the right face at the right time.

LESS MESS OPTION: Take photos of your child and you making happy and sad faces. Look at the photos together and say, "I am happy. I am sad." Then retell the story using your toddler's pictures for when the disciples are sad and happy.

JESUS CAME
BACK TO LIFE

He is
not here;
He
has
risen,
just as he said.
come and see
the place
where He lay.
matthew 28:6

GO ROUND
and round
the World

Go Round and Round the World
(to the tune of "The Farmer in the Dell")

Go round and round the world

Go round and round the world

Telling people about Jesus

Round and round the world

Replace 3rd line with:

– telling people Jesus died

– telling people He rose again

Hand Motions:

- GO – 2 arms pointing forward
- ROUND – roll arms in front of body
- THE WORLD – big circle with your arms
- TELLING – hands cupped around mouth
- PEOPLE – point to each other
- JESUS – arms out to side like cross

Hear and Learn: Jesus Tells His Disciples to Preach About Him

Jesus – arms out to the side like Jesus on the cross

After **Jesus** died on the **cross** (arms out to side) and came back to **life**, (jump up) **Jesus** went back to **heaven** (point up). But, before **Jesus** left to go back to **heaven**, He gave His **disciples** (point to people) some special **instructions** (count to 3 on your fingers). **Jesus** told them to **go** (pretend to run) **everywhere** (make a big circle with arms) and **tell** everyone about **Him**. The very last thing **Jesus** told His **disciples** was that they should **tell** everyone about Him.

What (hands up by shoulders like asking a question) kinds of things were they supposed to **tell** people? (Draw the following things or pause to sing the big truth songs from earlier in this book).

(1) God made Everything   (2) We are all Sinners

(3) Jesus Came to Earth   (4) Jesus Died on the Cross

(5) Jesus Came Back to Life

Jesus told His **disciples** to **tell** people about Him and when they did that, **lots** (point to several people) of people believed in **Jesus**. Just like **Jesus** told His first **disciples** to go **tell** everybody about Him, Jesus tells **us** (point to self) in the **Bible** (hold hands out like an open book) to **go** everywhere and **tell** everyone about **Him** (point up).

Play and Learn: Go and Tell!

Collect all of your child's cars, planes, trains and boats. Play together for several minutes. Talk about the cars driving on roads and boats traveling on water. Talk about using these things to get from one place to another. Remind them that Jesus said to go everywhere and tell everyone about Him. Fly the plane to your toddler and tell them a truth about Jesus. Then drive a car to them and do the same thing.

Memorize and Learn: Acts 1:8

- **But you** – point to someone else
- **will receive power** – make strong arms
- **when the Holy Spirit** – point up
- **comes on you;** – motion to come
- **and you will be my witnesses** – hand by mouth like puppet speaking
- **in Jerusalem,** – 2 hands parallel and close together
- **and in all Judea and Samaria,** – 2 hands move further apart
- **and to the ends of the earth.** – 2 hands move as far apart as you can
- **Acts 1:8**

Eat and Learn: Apple Boats

You will need: 1 apple, 4 pretzel sticks and a slice of cheese.

Remind your toddler that Jesus told His friends to go everywhere and tell people about Him. Tell them that one of the ways Jesus' friends would have traveled was on a boat. Pretend to be on a boat and go up and down on waves.

Cut apple into quarters and use a small knife to cut out the core. Place apples skin down on a plate. Have your toddler help you push a pretzel stick into each of the apple pieces. Cut the cheese slice into 4 triangles. Press the cheese onto the pretzel sticks as a sail. While your toddler eats their snack, review the things Jesus said His people should go and tell everyone.

Create and Learn: Paper Plate World

You will need: a paper plate, torn pieces of blue and green paper and a glue stick.

LESS MESS OPTION: Computer or phone.

On the paper plate, rough sketch a map of the world (use the next page for a template). Fill the continents with glue and have your toddler glue the green paper on the continents. As they work talk about how these are all the places in the world where people live. Remind them that Jesus told His disciples to go everywhere and tell everyone about Jesus. Talk about the different things we could tell someone about Jesus. Glue the remaining areas of the plate and have them stick the blue paper on the water areas. Explain that some of the first people to travel and tell others about Jesus went by boat across the water. Use your finger to make an imaginary boat go from one continent to another. Take a minute to pray for the people in other places who have never heard about Jesus.

LESS MESS OPTION: Look online for pictures of people in different countries around the world–even your own country/culture. Show them to your toddler and say things like, "See this man from India/France/America. People in India/France/America need to learn about Jesus." Then have your toddler tell the man in the picture something about Jesus.

Go tell Everyone about JESUS!

"But you will receive

power

when the Holy Spirit comes

on  ; and  will be

you   you

my witnesses in Jerusalem,

and in all Judea and Samaria,

and to the ends of the

 ." Acts 1:8

earth

APPENDIX

The Gospel-Centered Nursery

What were your main considerations when setting up your baby's nursery? Assuming you're like the average new parent, your first thought was of the color for the walls or the theme of the room. You wanted the room to appeal to your child. Then, you read reviews on furniture, purchased, put it together and sanitized it well. You wanted it to be safe and clean. Finally, you filled it with all the personal touches, like clothes and toys and books. The average new parent spends the whole 9 months and a few thousand dollars fitting out the nursery.

But, one thing often gets overlooked in nursery design and that is the soul of the baby you're getting ready to bring into that room. It's all too easy to get caught up in latest trends and meeting the physical needs of your baby – crying, feeding, diaper changing, etc. These are all crucial tasks, but sometimes in the midst of all the need meeting, we forget the biggest need – we forget the hearts of the babies and our own hearts and get caught up in the tasks of the moment.

In the pages that follow you'll find tools to help you remember the gospel while going about the tasks of raising your little one. Let these everyday objects and moments stand as memorials of truth and let them encourage you to stay focused on the truth of the gospel. And, as you remember the gospel in the mundane moments of your ministry in the nursery, use these gospel reminders to pray for the child God has entrusted to you.

Throughout the Bible we have examples of God telling His people to establish memorials. These were to stand as reminders of the goodness of God and His deliverance of His people.

In Deuteronomy 6:6-9 we read: "These commandments that I give you today are to be on your hearts. Impress them on your children. Talk about them when you sit at home and when you walk along the road, when you lie down and when you get up. Tie them as symbols on your hands and bind them on your foreheads. Write them on the doorframes of your houses and on your gates."

In this passage, God is giving His people instructions on how to remember the law by physically writing it on the doors of their houses, wearing it on their bodies and repeating it everywhere they went. If we're thinking about and talking about and seeing something, it's pretty hard for us to forget it.

And in Joshua 4:4-7 in the account of the people of Israel crossing the Jordan river in to the promised land, we read, "So Joshua called together the twelve men he had appointed from the Israelites, one from each tribe, and said to them, "Go over before the ark of the LORD your God into the middle of the Jordan. Each of you is to take up a stone on his shoulder, according to the number of the tribes of the Israelites, to serve as a sign among you. In the future, when your children ask you, 'What do these stones mean?' tell them that the flow of the Jordan was cut off before the ark of the covenant of the LORD. When it crossed the Jordan, the waters of the Jordan were cut off. These stones are to be a memorial to the people of Israel forever."

God commanded the people to build a structure of 12 stones for the sole purpose of remembering what God did that day and telling the next generation of God's deliverance. God even tells them that their children will ask about the stones and then they can tell them how the waters of the river parted, and God led them through on dry land. God knows that we are a forgetful people. Way back in the garden, Adam and Eve forgot, or chose to ignore, God's law. If we don't make a point of remembering something, we will forget it. With that in mind, here are five common items that are most surely in your child's nursery and how you can use them to point your child to Christ and to preach the gospel to your own heart.

Blanket:

As you wrap a little one up for sleep, remember two important truths. First, no matter how tired you (or the baby) are, you can trust that God never sleeps. Isaiah 40:28 tells us that, "He does not faint or grow weary." And, Psalm 121:4 tells us, "Indeed, he who watches over Israel will neither slumber nor sleep." What a great reminder as your weariness sets in.

Secondly, this blanket can serve as a reminder that God is sovereign over our sleeping and waking and He gives rest – both physical, in the form of sleep, and eternal, as those of us in Christ know we can rest in Him for our eternal salvation. Psalm 139:2 reminds us, "You know when I sit down and when I rise; you perceive my thoughts from afar." God knows that this little one needs to sleep, and He is sovereign over this moment.

Take a moment to pray for your child that he would grow to rely on God for his rest, both physically and spiritually, and that he would learn to run to Christ first in times of trouble.

Diapers:

During their first year of life, your little one will go through 2,500 to 3,000 diapers. Even if you're really quick (let's say 3 minutes), you will spend at least 125 hours or 5.2 whole days changing diapers before your child's first birthday.

Even in this most mundane moment of caring for your baby, you can remember the character of God and tremendous truths about your salvation. As you change your precious baby's diaper, instead of focusing on the smell or how it's the fifth stinky diaper of the day, take a moment to focus on the transformation that's taking place. The baby on the changing table in front of you is wallowing in his own filth and through no effort of his own, he is being made clean. Does this remind you of anything else?

When was the last time that you took time to meditate on your own salvation? If you are in Christ, you were once wallowing in your own filth – in the stench of your sin. Psalm 51:2 reminds us of this truth when it says, "Wash away all my iniquity and cleanse me from my sin." The truth a diaper change can remind you of, is that once you were dirty and helpless and unable to do anything about your filth, heading toward destruction. But, God in His great mercy acted through Christ and changed you, made you into a new creation and made you clean and spotless in His sight.

As you change your child's diaper, pause to thank God for your own salvation and pray for your child that they would come to see their own sin at an early age and turn to Christ for salvation. Pray that God would reveal Himself to them and help to see that they can't be good enough to change themselves, but that they need to rely on Christ in all things.

Baby Clothes:

Following on from being made clean in Christ, we can use the clothes that your baby is wearing as a reminder of how we are clothed in Christ and His righteousness.

Romans 13:14 says, "Rather, clothe yourselves with the Lord Jesus Christ, and do not think about how to gratify the desires of the flesh." And Isaiah 61:10 tells us, "I delight greatly in the Lord; my soul rejoices in my God. For he has clothed me with garments of salvation and arrayed me in a robe of his righteousness, as a bridegroom adorns his head like a priest, and as a bride adorns herself with her jewels."

Our clothing shows the world who we are. Each time you dress your little one, think about how you have been clothed. Just like God shed blood to make garments of skin to cover Adam and Eve in the garden, Christ's blood was shed to cover our sin and clothe us with His righteousness.

If you are in Christ, when they world sees you, they should see Christ and we can rejoice in the truth that when God the Father looks on us, He sees the righteousness of His Son and not our sin.

Pause and pray for your child to understand that unless Christ clothes him in righteousness he'll never be able to stand in the presence of God. Pray for yourself that you would live your life in a way that puts Christ on display for your children and the watching world to see.

Bottle and Bib (Feeding time):

Food is a regular part of all of our lives. Both you and your baby need to eat regularly. No matter how much you eat at one meal, within a few hours your body will be telling you to eat again. Our regular need for food is a built-in reminder of our dependence on God as the Great Provider.

Throughout the Bible we see example after example of God meeting the physical needs of His people ... Water from a rock, bread from heaven, a boy's lunch feeding 5000+. God is a God who meets the needs of His people. He perfectly meets our needs and sometimes even meets the needs we don't know we have. The next time you're feeding your little one, think about their dependence on you and then think about your dependence on God.

Not only does God meet our physical needs, most importantly He has met our greatest need of forgiveness and salvation through Christ. Romans 5:6 tells us, "You see, at just the right time, when we were still powerless, Christ died for the ungodly." God didn't wait for us to ask to be saved or to be ready to be saved, He acted on our behalf in a way we could never imagine or hope for. He paid the price for our sin. And now we live in dependence on Him knowing there is nothing more we can do to gain our salvation. He has done it all.

As you feed your little one, take a minute to thank God for the awesome way He has met your needs through the gift of Christ. Then, pray that your little one would trust in God alone to meet all of their needs. Thank God for entrusting you with this child and allowing you to be the one to point them to Christ and pray that you would be able to teach them to rely on Christ for all things.

Toys:

One final reminder is the simple toys you have chosen to entertain and educate your child. Let's be honest, there's nothing more precious than the laughter of a child. Laughter and joy are great gifts from God.

In those moments where you are tired and feeling helpless or weak, when the day seems like it will never end and you and your baby are tired and cranky, remember the laughter of a child and use that joy to remind you of the joy we have in Christ alone. Psalm 16:11, says, "You make known to me the path of life; you will fill me with joy in your presence, with eternal pleasures at your right hand." In God's presence there is fullness of joy. He knows and is sovereign over all you're going through right now, and His joy is complete.

Pause and thank God for the joy you have in Christ and pray that you would be faithful in proclaiming Him to your little bundle of joy. Let me encourage you not to be swayed by the things of the world, but to rejoice in Christ each and every day.

In Christ alone, our hope and our joy are found.

Other Scripture Texts/ Stories to Teach the Big Truths:

1. The Bible is God's Word
   - God's Word is Forever – 1 Peter 1:25
   - God's Word is a lamp to my feet – Psalm 119
2. God Made Everything
   - Creation points to God – Psalm 19
   - Jesus is the Word – John 1:1-3
3. We Are All Sinners
   - Noah and the Flood – Genesis 6-9
   - The Tower of Babel – Genesis 11
4. Only One God
   - Moses and the Burning Bush – Exodus 3
   - The Ark in the Temple of Dagon – 1 Samuel 5
5. God is Good
   - Abraham and Isaac – Genesis 22
   - Noah and the Flood – Genesis 6-9
6. Jesus Came to Earth
   - Jesus humbled Himself – Philippians 2:5-11
7. Jesus is the Son of God
   - Boy Jesus in the Temple – Luke 2:41-52
8. Jesus Died on the Cross
   - Prophesies of Jesus' Death – Isaiah 53
9. Jesus Came Back to Life
   - Jesus on the Road to Emmaus – Luke 24:13-35
   - Jesus Appears to His Disciples – Luke 24:36-49
10. Go Round and Round the World
   - Paul tells People About Jesus – Acts 17
   - Paul's Shipwreck – Acts 27-28

Using These Materials in a Church Setting

1. For a classroom setting, these materials are best used with ages 0-2 and could be stretched to include up to 3-year-old children.

2. Each Big Truth chapter could be taught as a stand-alone lesson. You could choose to use the whole lesson at once, going through the materials for 10 weeks and then rotating back through them, or you could spread the lessons out and spend 3 weeks on each lesson (see the chart below).

3. If you choose to spread the materials out over 30 weeks, each week you could teach the story, song and Bible verse along with one additional activity as shown below.

4. For classroom settings, be sure to check with parents about food allergies prior to the "eat and learn" activities.

5. Another option for using these in a church setting would be to use the story, song and memory verse at church and send the other activities home for parents to use during the week.

	Week 1	Week 2	Week 3
The Bible is God's Word	[car]	[eat]	[craft]
God Made Everything	[eat]	[craft]	[car]
We Are All Sinners	[craft]	[eat]	[car]
Only One God	[car]	[craft]	[eat]
God is Good	[car]	[eat]	[craft]
Jesus Came to Earth	[eat]	[craft]	[car]
Jesus is the Son of God	[car]	[craft]	[eat]
Jesus Died on the Cross	[craft]	[car]	[eat]
Jesus Came Back to Life	[eat]	[craft]	[car]
Go Round and Round the World	[craft]	[car]	[eat]

Allergy Alert!

Today we'll be tasting

_____

Please inform teachers of any known food allergies.

Bethany Darwin

Bethany is a full-time homemaker who recently "retired" from children's ministry after serving for twenty years in four different churches, including most recently thirteen years at the United Christian Church of Dubai. She is a graduate of Samford University where she studied Human Development and Family Studies (BA – 1997) and Southwestern Baptist Theological Seminary (MA in Christian Education – Children's Ministry – 2000). She loves to write materials to help children better understand the gospel, has written for several publications and has several books in the plans in the near future. She also spends a lot of her free time writing a food blog and playing with their one-year-old son.

Endorsements

Bethany Darwin has an amazing gift for creatively placing big truths in settings that make it easy and very enjoyable for children to see and appreciate just what those truths are. The songs and activities she has devised will delight not only the children, but the parents who will be thrilled to be able to use such an attractive and reliable guide book. I am deeply grateful for the background of ministry Bethany brings to her labors of love, and I pray many will benefit much as these same glorious big truths impact yet another generation, for God's glory and the growth and joy of our children.

Bruce A. Ware, Professor of Christian Theology, The Southern Baptist Theological Seminary, Author of Big Truths for Young Hearts

Bethany Darwin was children's ministry coordinator at our church, the United Christian Church of Dubai, for 13 years. We're so thankful that she came alongside parents to teach their children big truths about God during those years. Her love for children and heart for parents shows through in Sing and Play Big Truths. What a fun way to get weighty doctrine into the minds and souls of toddlers! We heartily recommend this book.

John and Keri Folmar, John is the Senior Pastor of the United Christian Church of Dubai. Keri, his wife, has written The Good Portion: Scripture.

Bethany is a gifted, God-centered teacher. I can't think of a better use of her extraordinary skills than equipping parents and teachers to lead the littlest souls among us. Bethany's ability to help us keep focused on Christ as we teach the Bible to children is not to be taken for granted. Sing and Play Big Truths is clear, creative, and fun – a great resource to bless our little brothers and sisters in Christ.

Gloria Furman, author of Treasuring Christ When Your Hands Are Full and Missional Motherhood

Biblical. Practical. Inspirational. Through this resource, Bethany leverages her 25+ years of formal children's ministry experience for the parent, guardian, nursery worker or Sunday school teacher looking to redeem the little years. As a pastor and as a parent of five, I particularly valued the clarity on the gospel and the age-appropriate strategies for sharing the gospel with this age group. This tool gives hope to all who long to live out the principles of Deuteronomy 6:4-6 in a practical way.

Justin Harris, Senior Pastor, Faith Bible Church, Naples, Florida

Experienced in leading children's ministry in churches for over 20 years, Bethany Darwin is an expert at equipping parents with the tools and ideas they need to nurture their children's understanding and excitement about God. She takes foundational truths and makes them fun and engaging for children without losing the truth. What better way is there to encourage your child's heart to learn and digest the truths of the gospel from a very young age? Definitely a needed resource for parents!

Kate Nel, homeschool mom of three toddlers

Bethany's book, "Sing and Play Big Truths" is a practical, reusable, fun tool to teach your children gospel truths through reading, singing, playing and even cooking together! It would be great to use in the home, at church or given as a gift. We wish we had a multi-purpose resource like this when my kids were younger.

John Welkner, Associate Pastor, United Christian Church of Dubai

We are very excited to see the culmination of Bethany's years in children's ministry make its way into a hands-on, reusable and fun teaching tool. As parents of four children and with over fifteen years of youth ministry experience, we understand the importance of teaching Gospel truths at a young age. Repetition is necessary. Involving multiple senses is essential. Teaching real truths, straight from the Bible is critical. Bethany's unique and creative book, "Sing and Play Big Truths", is unlike any other resource available. It encompasses it all. This book can be used in your home, at church and given as a gift. We are thrilled for the many opportunities families will have to learn Big Truths.

John and Lisa Welkner, John is an Associate Pastor at the United Christian Church of Dubai and Lisa is a homeschool mom and Ladies Bible study teacher.

CHRISTIAN FOCUS PUBLICATIONS

Christian Focus | Christian Heritage | CF4K | Mentor

Christian Focus Publications publishes books for adults and children under its four main imprints: Christian Focus, CF4K, Mentor and Christian Heritage. Our books reflect our conviction that God's Word is reliable and Jesus is the way to know him, and live for ever with him.

Our children's publication list includes a Sunday School curriculum that covers pre-school to early teens, and puzzle and activity books. We also publish personal and family devotional titles, biographies and inspirational stories that children will love.

If you are looking for quality Bible teaching for children then we have an excellent range of Bible stories and age-specific theological books.

From pre-school board books to teenage apologetics, we have it covered!

**Find us at our web page:
www.christianfocus.com**

CF4∙K
Because you're never too young to know Jesus

LITERACY FOR AGES 7-8

Ten Minute Tests

CONTENTS

Louis Fidge

A **prefix** is a group of letters we put **in front** of a word.
Prefixes **change the meaning** of the word.

Colour in your score on the testometer!

well

unwell

Choose the prefix un or dis to complete each word.

1. _____pack

2. _____well

3. _____place

4. _____trust

5. _____fair

6. _____happy

7. _____agree

8. _____may

9. _____load

10. _____bolt

11. _____honest

12. _____do

13. _____arm

14. _____charge

15. _____cover

15
14
13
12
11
10
9
8
7
6
5
4
3
2
1

A **verb** tells us what someone **is doing** or what **is happening**.

Colour in your score on the testometer!

Anna **is riding** her bike.

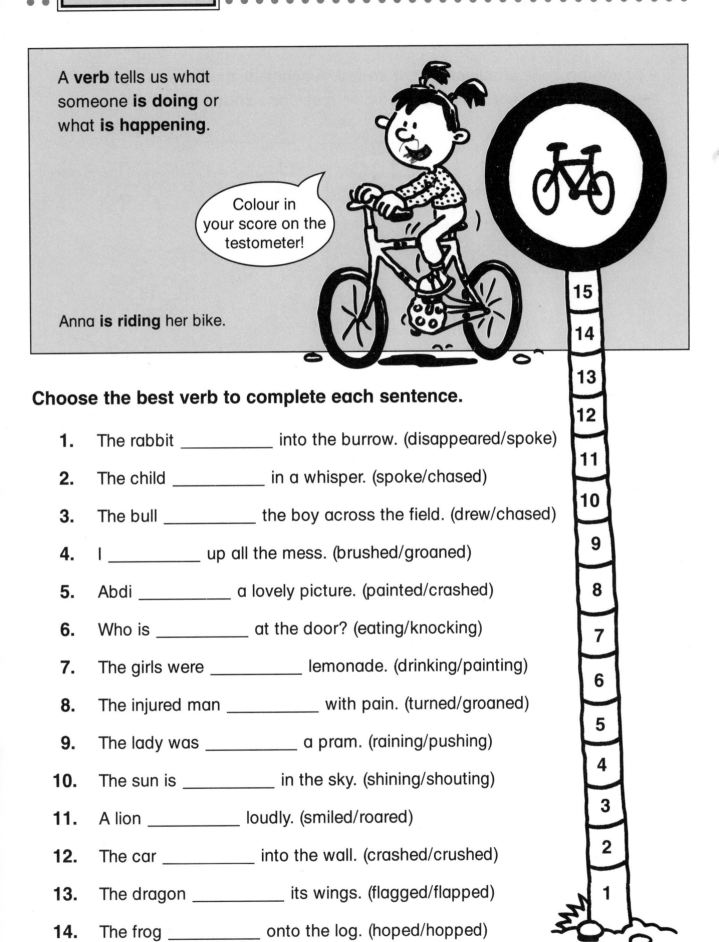

Choose the best verb to complete each sentence.

1. The rabbit _____ into the burrow. (disappeared/spoke)

2. The child _____ in a whisper. (spoke/chased)

3. The bull _____ the boy across the field. (drew/chased)

4. I _____ up all the mess. (brushed/groaned)

5. Abdi _____ a lovely picture. (painted/crashed)

6. Who is _____ at the door? (eating/knocking)

7. The girls were _____ lemonade. (drinking/painting)

8. The injured man _____ with pain. (turned/groaned)

9. The lady was _____ a pram. (raining/pushing)

10. The sun is _____ in the sky. (shining/shouting)

11. A lion _____ loudly. (smiled/roared)

12. The car _____ into the wall. (crashed/crushed)

13. The dragon _____ its wings. (flagged/flapped)

14. The frog _____ onto the log. (hoped/hopped)

15. A letter _____ through the letter box. (came/screamed)

15
14
13
12
11
10
9
8
7
6
5
4
3
2
1

A **phoneme** is the **smallest unit of sound**. A phoneme may be made up of **one or more letters** which make **one sound**.

b + oa + t = boat

This word is made by using three phonemes.

Choose the correct phoneme to complete each word.

1. m_____n (oo/ir)

2. tr_____t (ee/ea)

3. gr_____ (ow/oo)

4. gl_____ (ue/oo)

5. r_____d (oa/ow)

6. cl_____ (aw/ow)

7. p_____nt (au/ai)

8. b_____n (ir/ur)

9. _____l (ay/ow)

10. th_____sty (oo/ir)

11. yesterd_____ (ai/ay)

12. narr_____ (ow/aw)

13. r_____nd (ow/ou)

14. s_____cer (ou/au)

15. b_____l (oi/oa)

There are lots of words that end in **le**.

Colour in your score on the testometer!

a sin**gle** eag**le**

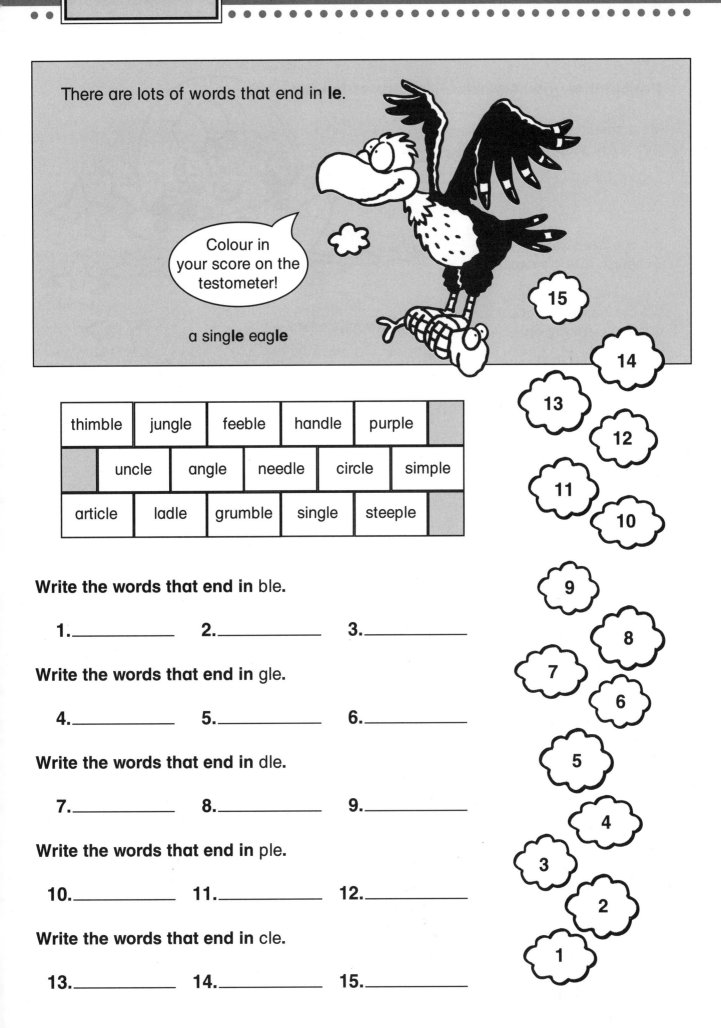

thimble	jungle	feeble	handle	purple	
uncle	angle	needle	circle	simple
article	ladle	grumble	single	steeple	

Write the words that end in ble.

1._____   2._____   3._____

Write the words that end in gle.

4._____   5._____   6._____

Write the words that end in dle.

7._____   8._____   9._____

Write the words that end in ple.

10._____   11._____   12._____

Write the words that end in cle.

13._____   14._____   15._____

Punctuation marks make writing **easier to read**.

Most sentences end with a **full stop**.

This is an alien.

If it is a **question**, a **question mark** is needed.

What is this?

We put an **exclamation mark** when we **feel strongly** about something.

What a strange alien!

Put in the missing punctuation mark in each sentence.

1. Where do you come from

2. What a funny name

3. The spaceship landed

4. A door opened slowly

5. Run for your life

6. Who is there

7. What do you want

8. It's not fair

9. This is terrible

10. The sun set in the sky

11. The bees buzzed near the flowers

12. How did the car crash

13. When did the letter come

14. Stop that at once

15. We have sausages and chips for tea

Colour in your score on the testometer!

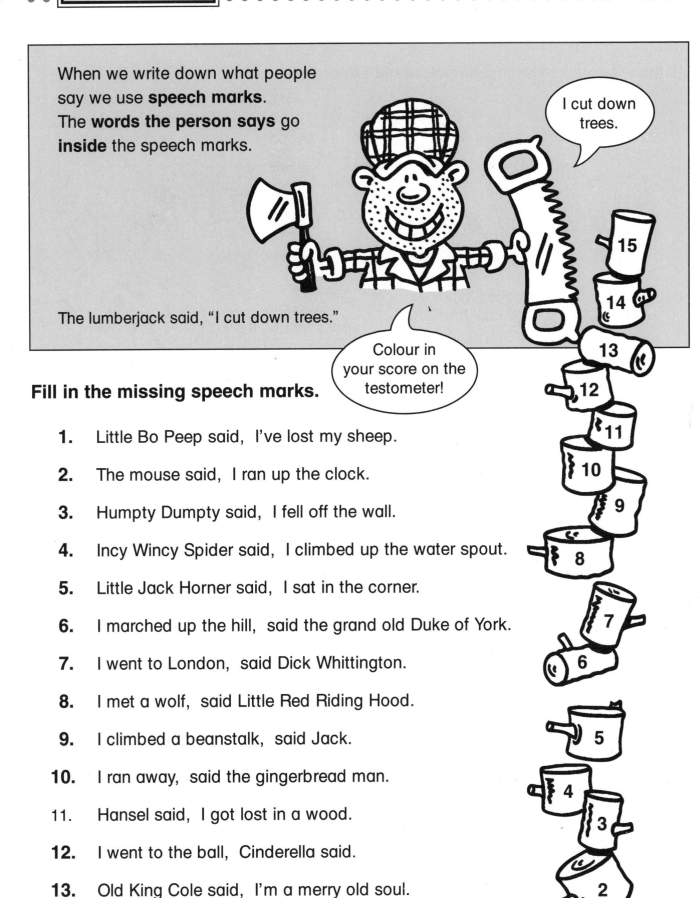

When we write down what people say we use **speech marks**. The **words the person says** go **inside** the speech marks.

I cut down trees.

The lumberjack said, "I cut down trees."

Colour in your score on the testometer!

Fill in the missing speech marks.

1. Little Bo Peep said, I've lost my sheep.

2. The mouse said, I ran up the clock.

3. Humpty Dumpty said, I fell off the wall.

4. Incy Wincy Spider said, I climbed up the water spout.

5. Little Jack Horner said, I sat in the corner.

6. I marched up the hill, said the grand old Duke of York.

7. I went to London, said Dick Whittington.

8. I met a wolf, said Little Red Riding Hood.

9. I climbed a beanstalk, said Jack.

10. I ran away, said the gingerbread man.

11. Hansel said, I got lost in a wood.

12. I went to the ball, Cinderella said.

13. Old King Cole said, I'm a merry old soul.

14. I made some tarts, said the Queen of Hearts.

15. I'm very ugly, the troll said.

Many books are arranged in **alphabetical order**.

These words are arranged in alphabetical order according to their **second** letter.

anteater   **b**ear   **c**amel   **d**eer   **d**og   **d**uck

These words are arranged in alphabetical order according to their **first** letter.

Colour in your score on the testometer!

Order these words according to their first letter.

1.   bat dog cat   _____

2.   goat elephant fox   _____

3.   hen kangaroo jaguar   _____

4.   ostrich monkey lion   _____

5.   rat seal penguin   _____

6.   zebra swan panda   _____

7.   hamster mouse donkey beetle   _____

8.   ox worm donkey giraffe   _____

Order these words according to their second letter.

9.   crab cow cat   _____

10. bird bull bear   _____

11. parrot pike pelican   _____

12. shark sardine snake   _____

13. trout tiger turtle toad   _____

14. giraffe gnu goat gerbil   _____

15. bee badger bird buffalo   _____

15
14
13
12
11
10
9
8
7
6
5
4
3
2
1

This is happening **now**, so the verb is in the **present tense**.

This happened in the **past**, so the verb is in the **past tense**.

Join up each verb with its past tense.

1. walk   hopped
2. hop   moved
3. carry   copied
4. move   walked
5. arrive   held
6. beg   carried
7. copy   spoke
8. hold   wrote
9. bring   came
10. see   taught
11. speak   arrived
12. take   brought
13. teach   took
14. write   begged
15. come   saw

Colour in your score on the testometer!

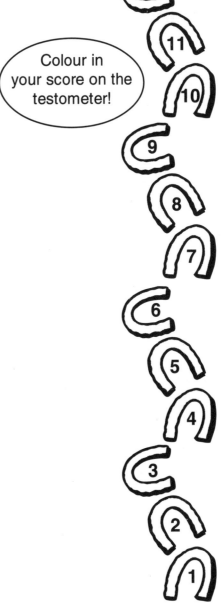

We use **commas** to **separate items in a list**.
We do **not** usually put a comma before the word **and**.

Colour in your score on the testometer!

Out of the window I saw a bus, a car, a van and a lorry.

Put in the missing commas in these sentences.

1. My friends are Sam Emma Abdi and Shanaz.

2. March June May and July are months of the year.

3. I like red blue yellow and green.

4. The four seasons are spring summer autumn and winter.

5. I have a dog a cat a fish and a budgie.

6. I hate sprouts cabbage parsnips and leeks.

7. I would like a bike a pen a book and a bag for Christmas.

8. Art science music and maths are good subjects.

9. In my bag I have a pen a ruler a rubber and a book.

10. London Rome Paris and Vienna are all capital cities.

11. I have been to France Spain Greece and Malta.

12. On the farm I saw some cows sheep pigs and hens.

13. On the rock there was a beetle an ant a slug and a snail.

14. Crisps chips chocolate and biscuits are not healthy.

15. In the sky you can see clouds the sun the moon and stars.

15
14
13
12
11
10
9
8
7
6
5
4
3
2
1

Test 10 Words inside words

If you look closely, sometimes you can see **small words inside longer words**.

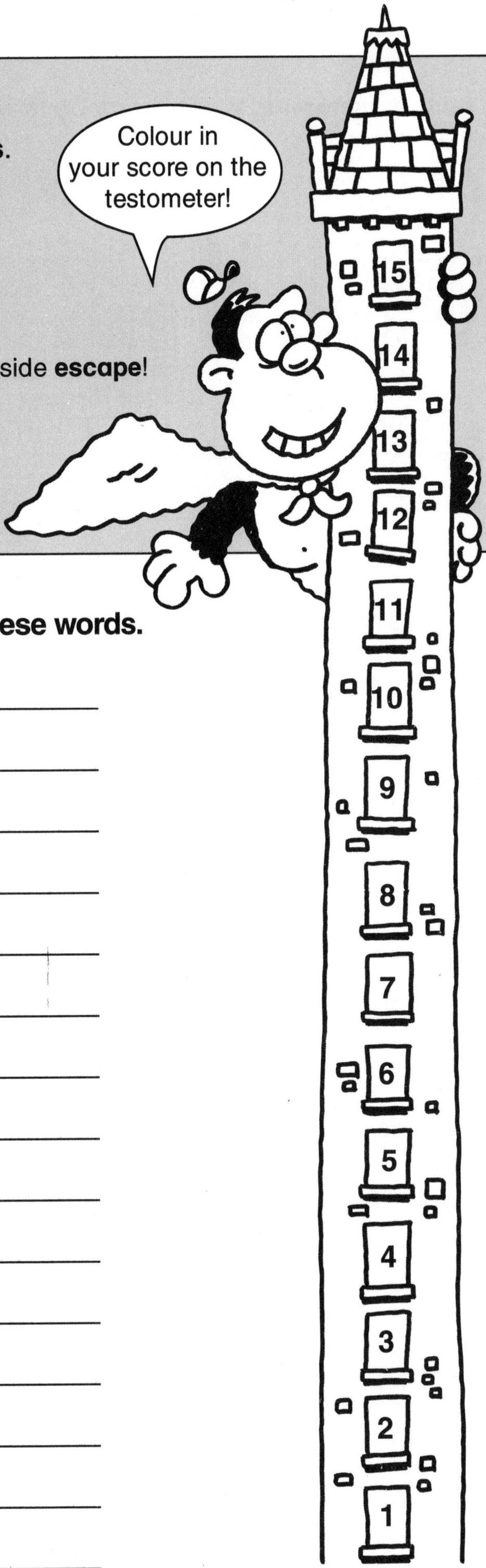

Colour in your score on the testometer!
15
14
13
12
11
10
9
8
7
6
5
4
3
2
1

There is an **ape** with a **cap** and a **cape** inside **escape**!

Find a small word 'hiding' in each of these words.

1. father ______________________
2. mother ______________________
3. heard ______________________
4. money ______________________
5. know ______________________
6. because ______________________
7. suddenly ______________________
8. friend ______________________
9. many ______________________
10. wheel ______________________
11. stage ______________________
12. question ______________________
13. narrow ______________________
14. rhyme ______________________
15. mystery ______________________

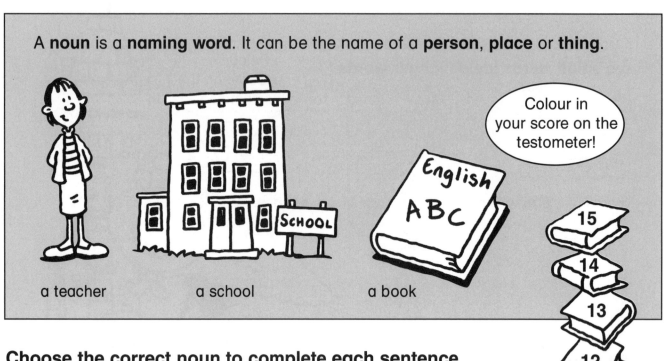

A **noun** is a **naming word**. It can be the name of a **person**, **place** or **thing**.

Colour in your score on the testometer!

a teacher   a school   a book

Choose the correct noun to complete each sentence.

1. A _____ makes things from wood. (mechanic/carpenter)

2. A _____ makes clothes. (tailor/grocer)

3. A _____ works on a farm. (baker/farmer)

4. A _____ rides horses in races. (diver/jockey)

5. An _____ looks after people's eyes. (doctor/optician)

6. Aeroplanes fly from an _____. (abbey/airport)

7. You can get petrol from a _____ . (garden/garage)

8. Ships load and unload at a _____. (dock/church)

9. We keep books in a _____. (lighthouse/library)

10. A _____ is where a king or queen lives. (palace/park)

11. We wash ourselves in a _____. (bed/sink)

12. A _____ is a baby's bed. (cot/cup)

13. Water is boiled in a _____.(knife/kettle)

14. We stir hot drinks with a _____. (spoon/stool)

15. Clothes are kept in a _____. (toaster/wardrobe)

A noun may be **singular** (when there is **only one** thing).
A noun may be **plural** when there is **more** than one thing).

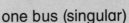
one bus (singular)

two buses (plural)

Colour in your score on the testometer!

**Complete these phrases.
Be careful with some of the spellings!**

1. one chair, lots of _____

2. one fox, lots of _____

3. one coach, lots of _____

4. one bush, lots of _____

5. one glass, lots of _____

6. one berry, lots of _____

7. one child, lots of _____

8. one man, lots of _____

9. one _____, lots of bikes

10. one _____, lots of boxes

11. one _____, lots of bunches

12. one _____, lots of dishes

13. one _____, lots of copies

14. one _____, lots of lorries

15. one _____, lots of sheep

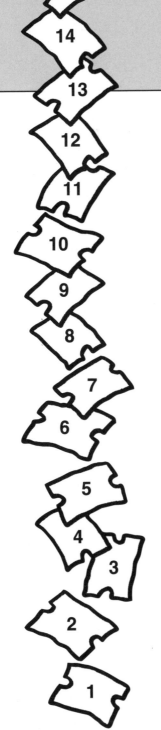

Some words contain **silent letters**. We cannot hear the letters when we say the words.

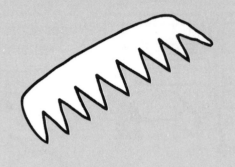

comb

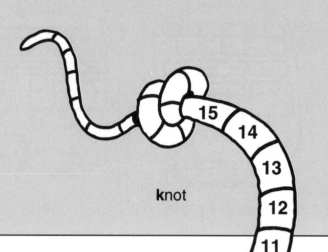

knot

Choose k **or** w **to complete each word.**

1. ____rite

2. ____nee

3. ____now

4. ____reck

5. ____rist

6. ____restle

7. ____nock

8. ____night

Choose b **or** g **to complete each word.**

9. num____

10. ____nat

11. clim____

12. crum____

13. thum____

14. ____nome

Colour in your score on the testometer!

15. ____naw

An **adjective** is a **describing** word. It tells us more about a **noun**.

Colour in your score on the testometer!

a **small** puppy

Choose the best adjective from the list below to go with each noun.

busy	handsome	dirty	old	beautiful	
	straight	sharp	heavy	funny	tall
open	muddy	loud	empty	fizzy	

1. a _____ weight   **2.** a _____ ruler

3. a _____ tree   **4.** a _____ clown

5. a _____ noise   **6.** a _____ puddle

7. a _____ mark   **8.** a _____ drink

9. an _____ door   **10.** a _____ road

11. an _____ glass   **12.** an _____ ruin

13. a _____ princess   **14.** a _____ knife

15. a _____ prince

A **suffix** is a **group of letters** we add to the **end** of a word.
A suffix changes the **meaning** of the word or the **job** the word does.

Colour in your score on the testometer!

power + ful
= powerful

power + less
= powerless

Add ful to the end of each word. Write the words you make.

1. colour _____

2. pain _____

3. care _____

4. thank _____

5. help _____

Add less to the end of each word. Write the words you make.

6. use _____

7. hope _____

8. thought _____

9. law _____

10. help _____

Take the suffix off each word. Write the words you are left with.

11. wonderful _____

12. heartless _____

13. graceful _____

14. faithless _____

15. pitiful _____

15
14
13
12
11
10
9
8
7
6
5
4
3
2
1

A **compound word** is a word made up of **two smaller words**.

Colour in your score on the testometer!

hand + bag = handbag

Do these word sums.

1. horse + shoe = _____

2. birth + day = _____

3. foot + step = _____

4. out + side = _____

5. with + out = _____

6. some + one = _____

7. grand + father = _____

8. hair + brush = _____

Write the two words that make up each of these compound words.

9. snowman _____ _____

10. motorway _____ _____

11. toothpaste _____ _____

12. cupboard _____ _____

13. eyesight _____ _____

14. wallpaper _____ _____

15. tablecloth _____ _____

The **subject** (the main person or thing) and the **verb** in each sentence must **agree**.

Colour in your score on the testometer!

The birds is flying. ☒

The birds are flying. ☑

Choose the correct form of the verb for each sentence.

1. Bells _____. (ring/rings)

2. The wind _____. (blow/blows)

3. A door _____. (open/opens)

4. Aeroplanes _____. (fly/flies)

5. An owl _____. (hoot/hoots)

6. Chickens _____ eggs. (lay/lays)

7. A rabbit _____ in a burrow. (live/lives)

8. Wolves _____. (howl/howls)

9. Mice _____. (squeak/squeaks)

10. I _____ my dinner. (eat/eats)

11. The children _____ to school. (go/goes)

12. Ben _____ a cold. (has/have)

13. The lady _____ some bread. (buy/buys)

14. Frogs _____. (hop/hops)

15. A cow _____ us milk. (give/gives)

15
14
13
12
11
10
9
8
7
6
5
4
3
2
1

A **collective noun** is the name given to a **group** of things.

a **herd** of cows

Colour in your score on the testometer!

| bunch | box | library | flock | swarm |
| chest | shoal | fleet | | |

Choose the best collective noun to complete each phrase.

1. a _____ of matches
2. a _____ of sheep

3. a _____ of bees
4. a _____ of drawers

5. a _____ of ships
6. a _____ of fish

7. a _____ of flowers
8. a _____ of books

| sticks | stones | singers | cornflakes |
| soldiers | trees | bananas | |

Choose the best word to complete each phrase.

9. a choir of _____
10. an army of _____

11. a packet of _____
12. a forest of _____

13. a bunch of _____
14. a bundle of _____

15. a pile of _____

15
14
13
12
11
10
9
8
7
6
5
4
3
2
1

We can classify adjectives according to type. These adjectives describe size.

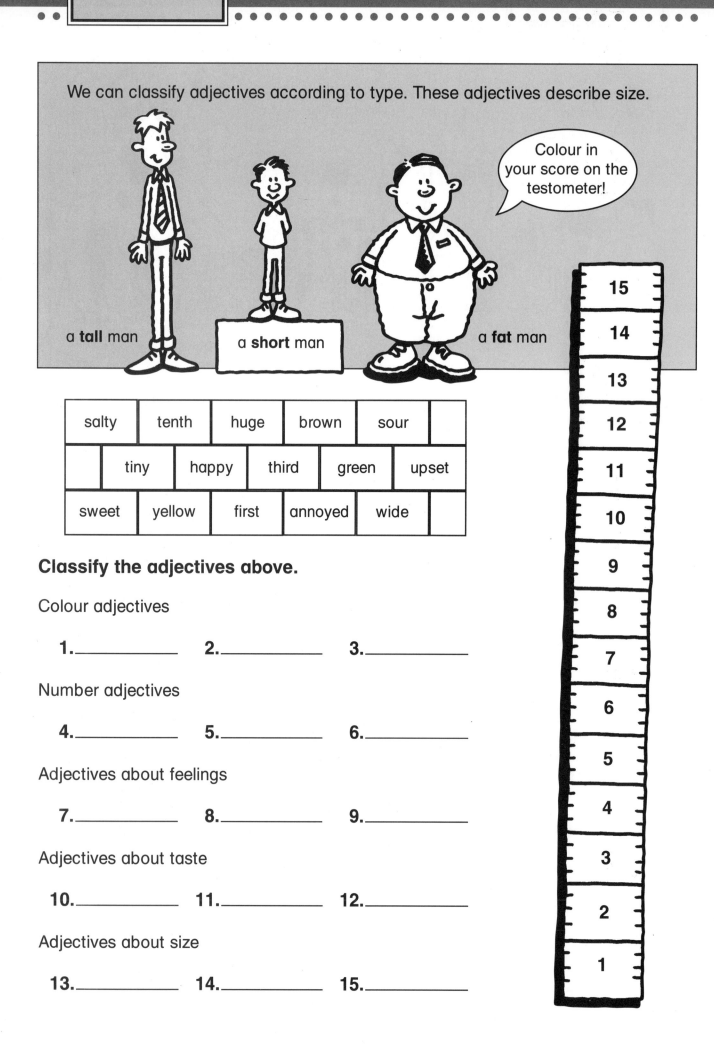

a **tall** man

a **short** man

a **fat** man

Colour in your score on the testometer!

salty	tenth	huge	brown	sour	
	tiny	happy	third	green	upset
sweet	yellow	first	annoyed	wide	

Classify the adjectives above.

Colour adjectives

1._____   2._____   3._____

Number adjectives

4._____   5._____   6._____

Adjectives about feelings

7._____   8._____   9._____

Adjectives about taste

10._____   11._____   12._____

Adjectives about size

13._____   14._____   15._____

When we say a word slowly, we can break it down into **smaller parts**. These parts are called **syllables**. Each syllable must contain at least **one vowel**.

Colour in your score on the testometer!

car
(one syllable)

lor + ry
(two syllables)

bull + do + zer
(three syllables)

Say these words slowly. Then write down if they have one, two or three syllables.

1. bus

2. jet

3. ambulance

4. hovercraft

5. ferry

6. drum

7. violin

8. rocket

9. trumpet

10. caravan

11. glider

12. coach

13. aeroplane

14. tractor

15. jeep

A **prefix** is a **group of letters** we put in front of a word. Prefixes **change the meaning** of the word.

Colour in your score on the testometer!

behave   **mis**behave

Choose the prefix re **or** pre **to begin each word.**

1. _____turn

2. _____heat

3. _____fix

4. _____view

5. _____pay

6. _____mind

7. _____fill

8. _____fund

Choose the prefix mis **or** ex **to begin each word.**

9. _____judge

10. _____handle

11. _____port

12. _____spell

13. _____lead

14. _____plode

15. _____pand

A **pronoun** is a word that takes the place of a **noun**.

Colour in your score on the testometer!

Ben cried when Ben hurt his leg.   Ben cried when **he** hurt his leg.

Choose the best pronoun to complete each sentence.

1. The lady went in the shop. _____ bought some apples. (He/She)

2. _____ am always busy. (We/I)

3. The boy shouted when _____ scored a goal. (he/they)

4. "Why are _____ late?" Mr Shah asked Abdi. (you/he)

5. "_____ are going to the park," the children said. (We/It)

6. _____ is a lovely day. (It/You)

7. Are _____ good at writing? (he/you)

8. _____ like playing games. (We/It)

9. The girl fell off her bike when _____ crashed. (she/you)

10. When the dog stopped _____ barked. (it/they)

11. The prince got up. _____ got dressed. (She/He)

12. I tried to lift the box but _____ was too heavy. (we/it)

13. When I shouted at the birds _____ flew away. (it/they)

14. The boy walked with the girl. _____ went in the park. (We/They)

15. When the man stopped _____ sat down. (you/he)

Antonyms are words that have the **opposite** meaning.

open

closed

Colour in your score on the testometer!

Join up the pairs of words with the opposite meaning.

1.	wild	white
2.	low	hot
3.	rough	tame
4.	black	bottom
5.	cheap	high
6.	cold	dear
7.	difficult	smooth
8.	wide	arrive
9.	top	empty
10.	first	easy
11.	near	left
12.	under	far
13.	depart	narrow
14.	right	over
15.	full	last

When we are writing about **ourselves** we write in the **first person**. We use pronouns like **I** and **we**.

When we are writing about **others** we write in the **third person**. We use pronouns like **he**, **she**, **it** and **they**.

I called for Ben.
We went swimming.

Annie and Lucy were surprised when **they** opened the box.

Colour in your score on the testometer!

Say if each of the pronouns marked in bold is in the first or third person.

1. **I** went to school. _____

2. Tom went out when **he** finished washing up. _____

3. The children chattered as **they** ate the bananas. _____

4. When the dog appeared **it** ran straight home. _____

5. The flowers looked lovely. **They** were all different colours. _____

6. **We** went to the cinema in the evening. _____

7. May **I** have some, please? _____

8. "**We** can do it!" Tom and Ben shouted. _____

9. The machine made a loud noise when **it** was turned on. _____

10. **I** am older than Sam. _____

11. Mr Shah went to bed. **He** went straight to sleep. _____

12. The lady was happy but **she** didn't smile. _____

13. **They** ran for the bus. _____

14. **I** was too frightened to move. _____

15. **We** all like to win games. _____

15
14
13
12
11
10
9
8
7
6
5
4
3
2
1

Push

A **conjunction** is a **joining word**.
It may be used to join **two sentences**.

Colour in your score on the testometer!

I picked up the comic. I read it.   I picked up the comic and read it.

Choose the best conjunction to complete each sentence.

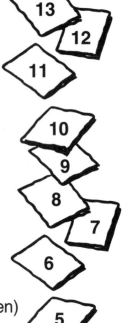

1. I had a bath _____ went to bed. (and/but)

2. An elephant is huge _____ an ant is small. (and/but)

3. I made a sandwich _____ ate it. (and/but)

4. Your towel is wet _____ mine is dry. (and/but)

5. A rabbit is fast _____ a snail is slow. (and/but)

6. I like swimming _____ playing rounders. (and/but)

7. You will get into trouble _____ you talk. (if/so)

8. I was wet _____ it was raining. (if/because)

9. It was hot _____ I took off my jumper. (so/because)

10. The door has been broken _____ I slammed it. (since/when)

11. I ran fast _____ I was late. (if/because)

12. We went for a walk _____ it was very hot. (so/although)

13. I will buy a lolly _____ you give me the money. (if/as)

14. You will get wet _____ you go in the rain. (if/so)

15. My uncle didn't come _____ I didn't see him. (so/if)

We can make new words by **changing** some letters.

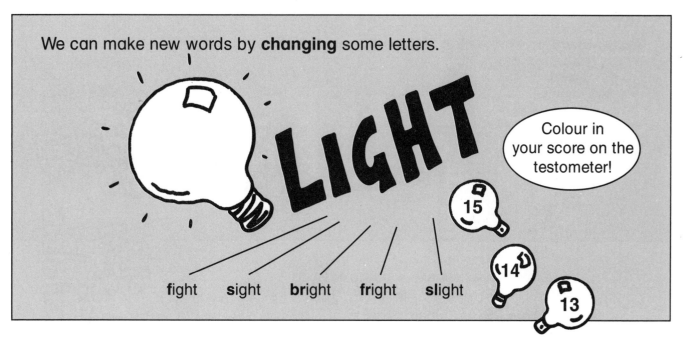

LIGHT

Colour in your score on the testometer!

fight   sight   **br**ight   **fr**ight   **sl**ight

Make some new words.

1. Change the **f** in **f**arm to **ch**. _____

2. Change the **d** in **d**ead to **thr**. _____

3. Change the **w** in **w**ay to **del**. _____

4. Change the **f** in **f**eed to **gr**. _____

5. Change the **n** in **n**erve to **sw**. _____

6. Change the **n** in **n**ew to **scr**. _____

7. Change the **d** in **d**irt to **squ**. _____

8. Change the **m** in **m**oan to **gr**. _____

9. Change the **v** in **v**oice to **ch**. _____

10. Change the **w** in **w**ood to **bl**. _____

11. Change the **l** in **l**oud to **pr**. _____

12. Change the **m** in **m**ow to **borr**. _____

13. Change the **c** in **c**urb to **dist**. _____

14. Change the **d** in **d**are to **bew**. _____

15. Change the **n** in **n**ear to **app**. _____

Possessive pronouns tell us who the **owner** of something is.

These are **my** toys. They are not **yours**. They are mine.

Colour in your score on the testometer!

> **Some common possessive pronouns are:**
> my   mine   your   yours   his   her   hers   its
> our   ours   their   theirs

Underline the possessive pronoun in each sentence.

1. This is my book.

2. The children picked up their bags.

3. The boy was sure the pen was his.

4. The girl lost her ruler.

5. The robot opened its mouth.

6. "You can't have the ball. It's ours!" Ben shouted.

7. The lady lost her way.

8. This book is mine.

9. We parked our car and got out.

10. I asked the girl if the pen was hers.

11. The ball had their name on it.

12. The children knew the toys were theirs.

13. "I like your picture best," the teacher said to Mary.

14. "Ali broke our model," Amy and Emma complained.

15. This bag belongs to you. It is yours.

Sometimes we **shorten** words and leave letters out. These words are called **contractions**. We use an **apostrophe** to show where letters are missing.

I've got an ice-cream.

Colour in your score on the testometer!

I've = I have

Put in the missing apostrophes in the correct places in these contractions.

1. Im

2. hes

3. Ive

4. wed

5. Ill

6. wouldnt

7. were

8. heres

9. doesnt

10. its

11. wasnt

12. whos

13. wont

14. dont

15. youre

When we write down what people say we use **speech marks**.
The **words the person says** go **inside** the speech marks.

Do you like my pet spider?

Colour in your score on the testometer!

Emma said, "Do you like my pet spider?"

Put in the missing speech marks in these sentences.

1. Hello, Ben said.

2. It's nice to see you, Sam replied.

3. What a lovely day! exclaimed Ben.

4. Yes it's so warm, Sam answered.

5. The weather forecast said it would rain, Ben said.

6. I don't think it will, Sam replied.

7. I can see a few black clouds, Ben commented.

8. I think they will pass over, Sam said.

9. Where are you off to? Ben asked.

10. I'm going to town to do some shopping, Sam answered.

11. May I come? Ben asked.

12. Yes, of course. Shall we walk or wait for a bus? Sam said.

13. Let's walk, Ben suggested.

14. I think I can feel a few spots of rain, Sam said.

15. Let's get the bus, then, said Ben.

A **proper noun** is a **special** (or **particular**) name of a **person**, **place** or **thing**. Proper nouns always begin with a **capital letter**.

Colour in your score on the testometer!

AMERICA

New York

Here is **W**ayne.   **N**ew **Y**ork is in **A**merica.   This is the **E**mpire **S**tate **B**uilding.

Rewrite these proper nouns correctly.

1. anna   _____

2. mr khan   _____

3. doctor parker   _____

4. bert   _____

5. washington   _____

6. green park   _____

7. high street   _____

8. charing cross station   _____

9. daily mirror   _____

10. tottenham hotspur   _____

11. wednesday   _____

12. february   _____

13. christmas   _____

14. golden sands hotel   _____

15. moscow   _____

Answers

Test 1
The missing prefix is in **bold**.
1. **un**pack
2. **un**well
3. **dis**place
4. **dis**trust
5. **un**fair
6. **un**happy
7. **dis**agree
8. **dis**may
9. **un**load
10. **un**bolt
11. **dis**honest
12. **un**do
13. **dis**arm
14. **dis**charge
15. **un**cover

Test 2
1. disappeared
2. spoke
3. chased
4. brushed
5. painted
6. knocking
7. drinking
8. groaned
9. pushing
10. shining
11. roared
12. crashed
13. flapped
14. hopped
15. came

Test 3
The correct phoneme is in **bold**.
1. m**oo**n
2. tr**ea**t
3. gr**ow**
4. g**l**ue
5. r**oa**d
6. cl**aw**
7. p**ai**nt
8. b**ur**n
9. **ow**l
10. thi**r**sty
11. yesterd**ay**
12. narr**ow**
13. r**ou**nd
14. s**au**cer
15. b**oi**l

Test 4
1. thimble
2. feeble
3. grumble
4. jungle
5. angle
6. single
7. handle
8. needle
9. ladle
10. purple
11. simple
12. steeple
13. uncle
14. circle
15. article

Test 5
1. Where do you come from?
2. What a funny name!
3. The spaceship landed.
4. A door opened slowly.
5. Run for your life!
6. Who is there?
7. What do you want?
8. It's not fair!
9. This is terrible!
10. The sun set in the sky.
11. The bees buzzed near the flowers.
12. How did the car crash?
13. When did the letter come?
14. Stop that at once!
15. We have sausages and chips for tea.

Test 6
1. Little Bo Peep said, "I've lost my sheep."
2. The mouse said, "I ran up the clock."
3. Humpty Dumpty said, "I fell off the wall."
4. Incy Wincy Spider said, "I climbed up the water spout."
5. Little Jack Horner said, "I sat in the corner."
6. "I marched up the hill," said the grand old Duke of York.
7. "I went to London," said Dick Whittington.
8. "I met a wolf," said Little Red Riding Hood.
9. "I climbed a beanstalk," said Jack.
10. "I ran away," said the gingerbread man.
11. Hansel said, "I got lost in a wood."
12. "I went to the ball," Cinderella said.
13. Old King Cole said, "I'm a merry old soul."
14. "I made some tarts," said the Queen of Hearts.
15. "I'm very ugly," the troll said.

Test 7
1. bat cat dog
2. elephant fox goat
3. hen jaguar kangaroo
4. lion monkey ostrich
5. penguin rat seal
6. panda swan zebra
7. beetle donkey hamster mouse
8. donkey giraffe ox worm
9. cat cow crab
10. bear bird bull
11. parrot pelican pike
12. sardine shark snake
13. tiger toad trout turtle
14. gerbil giraffe gnu goat
15. badger bee bird buffalo

Test 8
1. walked
2. hopped
3. carried
4. moved
5. arrived
6. begged
7. copied
8. held
9. brought
10. saw
11. spoke
12. took
13. taught
14. wrote
15. came

Test 9
1. My friends are Sam, Emma, Abdi and Shanaz.
2. March, June, May and July are months of the year.
3. I like red, blue, yellow and green.
4. The four seasons are spring, summer, autumn and winter.
5. I have a dog, a cat, a fish and a budgie.
6. I hate sprouts, cabbage, parsnips and leeks.
7. I would like a bike, a pen, a book and a bag for Christmas.
8. Art, science, music and maths are good subjects.
9. In my bag I have a pen, a ruler, a rubber and a book.
10. London, Rome, Paris and Vienna are all capital cities.
11. I have been to France, Spain, Greece and Malta.
12. On the farm I saw some cows, sheep, pigs and hens.
13. On the rock there was a beetle, an ant, a slug and a snail.
14. Crisps, chips, chocolate and biscuits are not healthy.
15. In the sky you can see clouds, the sun, the moon and stars.

Test 10
1. fat (or) her (or) the
2. the (or) moth
3. ear (or) hear
4. one
5. now (or) no
6. use (or) be (or) cause (or) us
7. den
8. end
9. man (or) any (or) an
10. eel (or) heel
11. tag (or) age (or) stag
12. quest (or) on
13. row (or) arrow
14. me
15. my

Test 11
1. carpenter
2. tailor
3. farmer
4. jockey
5. optician
6. airport
7. garage
8. dock
9. library
10. palace
11. sink
12. cot
13. kettle
14. spoon
15. wardrobe

Test 12
1. chairs
2. foxes
3. coaches
4. bushes
5. glasses
6. berries
7. children
8. men
9. bike
10. box
11. bunch
12. dish
13. copy
14. lorry
15. sheep

Test 13
1. **w**rite
2. **k**nee
3. **k**now
4. **w**reck
5. **w**rist
6. **w**restle
7. **k**nock
8. **k**night
9. num**b**
10. **g**nat
11. clim**b**
12. crum**b**
13. thum**b**
14. **g**nome
15. **g**naw

Test 14
1. heavy
2. straight
3. tall
4. funny
5. loud
6. muddy
7. dirty
8. fizzy
9. open
10. busy
11. empty
12. old
13. beautiful
14. sharp
15. handsome

Test 15
1. colourful
2. painful
3. careful
4. thankful
5. helpful
6. useless
7. hopeless
8. thoughtless
9. lawless
10. helpless
11. wonder
12. heart
13. grace
14. faith
15. pity